BECOMING ALCOHOLIC

Alcoholics Anonymous and the Reality of Alcoholism

DAVID R. RUDY

SOUTHERN ILLINOIS UNIVERSITY PRESS
CARBONDALE AND EDWARDSVILLE

Library of Congress Cataloging in Publication Data

Rudy, David R.
  Becoming alcoholic.

  Bibliography: p.
  Includes index.
   1. Alcoholics—Middle Atlantic States—Case studies.
  2. Alcoholics Anonymous—Case Studies. I. Title.
  HV5297.M55R83   1986   362.2'9286   85-11750
  ISBN 0-8093-1244-1
  ISBN 0-8093-1245-X (pbk.)

FOR THE
MEMBERS OF
MIDEASTERN CITY
A.A.

CONTENTS

FOREWORD

D AVID R. RUDY'S *Becoming Al-
coholic* addresses a major social issue in our society: that form of
conduct called alcoholism, which touches the lives of one out of
seven Americans on a daily basis. Rudy examines the process by
which individuals who are seen by others as having problems with
alcohol come to define themselves as "alcoholics." Through treatment agencies, through the meetings and literature of Alcoholics
Anonymous (A.A.), and through interactions with significant others
and with persons who call themselves alcholics, the problem drinker
gradually takes on an alcoholic identity. Rudy shows how that identity derives from the ideological system of A.A., particularly from
A.A.'s conception of alcoholism as a disease. This conception received its strongest formulation in E. M. Jellinek's phase model, developed in the 1940s and 1950s and subsequently adopted by most
physicians and treatment agencies, by sociologists and psychologists
studying the problem, and by American society in general. Thus,
the disease model was refined within the scientific and everyday
worlds of discourse that most directly affect the problem drinker.

Emphasizing that the chemical ethyl alcohol will not by itself create an alcoholic, Rudy focuses on the process of alcoholic self-definition, how an individual becomes an alcoholic within the interpretive practices of our society. From this interactionist perspective, Rudy redefines alcoholism as a characterization attached to drinkers when others question their drinking behavior and when drinkers lack the power or desire to negotiate another explanation of that behavior. This cultural and interpretive view of alcoholism illuminates the phenomenon in a new way, for it stresses how society and its interactants shape the behaviors of problem drinkers. In particular, A.A. produces a new kind of interactant who, while learning how to call him- or herself alcoholic, also learns a new ideological and interpretive system regarding self, society, alcohol, and alcoholism. As Gregory Bateson has suggested, A.A. teaches a new epistemology and a new ontology, a new theory of being in the world.

By examining the processual, subjective, and situational features involved in becoming an alcoholic, Rudy joins a long and distinguished research tradition. Often associated with the Chicago School, this research method focuses on the individual's definition of his or her situation. Rudy's process model suggests that an individual may follow one of four paths or careers in becoming an alcoholic. This typology, which includes pure, convinced, converted, and tangential alcoholics, suggests that the label "alcoholic," as it is generally understood, is more readily attached to some individuals than to others. Rudy's typology also elaborates and deepens previous explanations that scholars such as Maxwell, Trice, Leach and Norris have offered concerning the process of affiliation with A.A.

Rudy's investigation thus contributes on four fronts. First, he takes us into the processes that influence the way an individual comes to accept an alcoholic characterization. Second, he analyzes A.A. as an interactional site within which this definition process occurs. Third, he reinterprets the meaning of alcoholism from the standpoint of the sociological approach to deviance, deviants, and social control agents. Fourth, he adds an important document to the qualitative research tradition associated with the symbolic interactionists. His use of open-ended interviews, participant observation, and limited case or life histories has permitted him to write a sensitive but probing analysis of the alcoholic experience.

It is apparent that our postcapitalist society is struggling with new interpretations of the terms "alcoholism," "drug addiction," and "chemical dependency." A new arm of the health care industry has arisen to process addicts and alcoholics. Treatment centers for alcoholics, once uncommon, now produce "recovering alcoholics" at a rapid rate. Some of these individuals turn up in A.A.; some gravitate to other worlds of recovery and interaction; some disappear altogether from the treatment field. Narcotics Anonymous has recently appeared, for many persons labeled alcoholics are also labeled drug addicts or chemical dependents—a new type of recovering deviant. Those who choose to follow Rudy's work will have to probe the historical, social, and institutional developments that continue to affect the meanings of these terms. How these meanings are structured and lived into existence will remain an area of intensive inquiry.

David Rudy's study takes its place in the small group of investigations aimed at a humanistic understanding of the lived experiences of those persons who have come to be called "alcoholic." His work is a required point of departure for all future research in this area. For this he is to be commended.

NORMAN K. DENZIN

PREFACE

ONE OF THE MOST anxiety-producing and yet most exciting aspects of doing field research is the uncertainty of direction. Rather than beginning a study with a specific question, most field research starts with a setting, an arena of social life, and it allows that setting, its participants, and the researcher's perception of these to forge themes, questions, hypotheses, and grounded theories. This study depicts some of my experiences and interpretations during sixteen months of participant observation in Alcoholics Anonymous (A.A.). I am not a member of A.A., nor have I ever been. For whatever difference it makes, I am also not an abstainer. I respect A.A. and its members, but I remain as critical and objective as possible in viewing, understanding, and analyzing the fellowship.

This research also reflects the accounts and interpretations of "Mideastern City" A.A. members who shared their "experience, strength, and hope" with me. To protect their anonymity, all names of cities, A.A. groups, and individuals within the text of the book are pseudonyms.

Finally, this book examines the relationship between the social construction of alcoholism by Mideastern City A.A. members and the construction of alcoholism by contemporary alcohologists. Just as Mideastern City A.A. members utilize A.A. ideology and their beliefs about alcoholism in interpreting their social world, so too do I utilize concepts, assumptions, and theoretical perspectives in organizing reality. Initial questions developed in the field reflect some of these underlying influences.

QUESTIONS

This study is organized around general questions. What are the processes involved in becoming an A.A. member and in becoming alcoholic? That is, how do people who approach A.A. come to be socially differentiated or defined by themselves and others as A.A. members and as alcoholics. In other words, how do people who make contact with A.A. become A.A. affiliates? In becoming A.A. members, prospective affiliates experience processes similar to what researchers in the sociology of religion call "conversion." That is, they radically change and reconstruct their identities, world views, and lives. In "becoming alcoholic," some individuals regard themselves as alcoholics before approaching A.A., but many do not identify with alcoholism until after affiliation with A.A. The focus upon "becoming" in this research emphasizes alcoholism as an emergent phenomenon. How A.A. members come to define themselves as alcoholics, how they talk about their alcoholism, and how alcoholic designations organize and give meaning to their lives are all important in "becoming alcoholic." A.A. alcoholics are different from other alcoholics, not because there are more "gamma alcoholics" or "alcohol addicts" in A.A., but because they come to see themselves and to reconstruct their lives by utilizing the views and ideology of A.A.

Becoming alcoholic and the type of alcoholic one becomes has as much to do with the responses of others—treatment agencies, psychiatrists, A.A., and friends—as it does with the drinking activities and life experiences of the persons labeled alcoholic. A.A. alcoholics come to reinterpret and give meaning to their past and current lives by adopting A.A. beliefs and roles. To suggest that, to a significant extent, becoming alcoholic is a subjective experience, a subjective reality, is not to make alcoholism less real than if it is looked at purely objectively as a disease characterized by blackouts, loss of control, increased tolerance, withdrawal symptoms, or whatever. Indeed, the objective reality around each of us pales when compared to subjective and symbolic realities. Many Mideastern City A.A. members constructed and experienced a reality in which alcohol and drinking became the dominant and exclusive features of their lives.

A second question probes the relationship of A.A. to dominant phase models and definitions of alcoholism in contemporary America. Just as A.A. members "construct" their alcoholism by attaching meanings, definitions, and interpretations to their experiences, so too do alcohologists construct alcoholism.

These initial questions, once formulated in the field, shaped data collection, but other serendipitous findings shaped the study as well. Frequent experiences of hearing and talking with A.A. members who had "slipped" led me to explore the functions of drinking within Mideastern City A.A.; and listening to the same members provide differing explanations of their alcoholism led to an analysis of the functions of disease and personal explanations of alcoholism for A.A. members.

This study differs substantially from other detailed accounts of A.A. members by social scientists (Gellman, 1964; Madsen, 1974; Kurtz, 1979; Robinson, 1979; Maxwell, 1984). *Becoming Alcoholic* has less organizational emphasis than these recent works do. Major attention is directed toward personal accounts—interviews, life-history interviews, and testimonials—to demonstrate how A.A. members engage in "constructing" or "reconstructing" their alcoholism. This work also goes beyond the previously completed studies in that some of the connections between A.A. ideology and alcoholism models and theories are explored. In other words, the reality of alcoholism in A.A. is used as a data source and a springboard to address the reality of alcoholism in contemporary America. Alcoholism is more a social and political accomplishment than a scientific accomplishment (Schneider, 1978). As in other qualitative research (Bogdan and Taylor, 1975), scientific studies and other relevant literature are integrated into those chapters where they relate closely to the argument.

ORGANIZATION

Throughout the first six chapters, my emphasis is directed toward ethnographic views of members' lives and experiences. This approach starts in chapter 1 with an organizational description of A.A. and moves to a discussion of the affiliation process with A.A. in chapter 2. Although there is some regional diversity between A.A. groups, I believe that Mideastern City A.A. is fairly typical of the fellowship in other urban areas. Other researchers' accounts of A.A. groups from New York to California, while different in style and emphasis, essentially describe processes similar to those described in this book. After an organizational analysis of A.A. and a discussion of the affiliation process, chapter 3 presents and analyzes members' accounts of their alcoholism. This analysis is continued in chapter 4 with the development of a typology of A.A. alcoholic careers. Chapter 5 describes slipping (drinking) within A.A. and its functions in relation to individual sobriety and group solidarity.

The final three chapters go well beyond the confines of the organization in exploring the relationship between the reality of alcoholism in A.A. and its reality in contemporary America. Chapter 6 examines the influence of A.A. ideology upon Jellinek's phase model of alcoholism. Chapter 7 discusses how alcoholism can be defined as an objective phenomenon as well as a label attached to a wide range of drinking behaviors and drinking problems. The chapter culminates with an interactionist definition of alcoholism drawn from labeling theory. Finally, chapter 8 uses A.A. slogans to organize much of the contemporary sociological literature on alcoholism and drinking problems.

ACKNOWLEDGMENTS

Duuring the long time that I have worked on this book, many friends and colleagues have helped me. Helpful during the early stages of the research were Bob Bogdan and Jerry Jacobs, who taught me and encouraged me to do participant observation; Bill Pooler, who loved to read and criticize my field notes; and particularly Hal Mizruchi, who always challenged me to put everything within a theoretical context. Other friends, particularly Bill Hall, Tom Leitko, Rich Switzer, and George Zito, have listened, questioned, and argued over the years, and despite my stubbornness, they are responsible for modifying and refocusing some of my thinking. Larry Greil made a similar contribution and also helped recast chapter 2; he is that chapter's coauthor. Special debt is also acknowledged to Gene Obidinski, who encouraged my sociological imagination in the first place.

More recently, other official and unofficial reviewers and critics deserve acknowledgment. Kai Erikson provided valuable comments for my discussion of drinking and its functions in Alcoholics Anonymous. Norman Denzin, Harry Trice, and Paul Roman constructively criticized some of my earlier journal work and this manuscript in its entirety. I have incorporated some of their suggestions and comments but have stubbornly resisted others—perhaps mistakenly. Leonard Blumberg and David Pittman, supporters and friends of mine in the Drinking and Drugs Division of the Society for the Study of Social Problems, have in less direct but very important ways engaged and affected my thinking and deserve acknowledgment.

Kenney Withers, director of Southern Illinois University Press, deserves special acknowledgment for the encouragement, support, and faith that he was able to communicate through numerous letters and phone conversations. Thanks also to Carolyn Hamilton, whose word-processing skills and humor have made writing and revising more enjoyable. My main debt of gratitude is to the members of Mideastern City A.A. who have shared themselves and their lives with me and who have affected this book and my views on many things. I also wish to acknowledge the understanding and support that my family, particularly my parents, Rose and Jim, and my children, Maura and Michael, have given me. Lastly and most importantly, Mary, my wife, has been my most important critic and friend, and she is responsible for making my life and work worthwhile.

Permission to quote from the following copyright sources is gratefully acknowledged:

The Twelve Steps and Twelve Traditions reprinted with permission of Alcoholics Anonymous World Services, Inc., copyrighted 1939, 1955, 1976.

The Preamble reprinted with permission of the A.A. *Grapevine.*

Chapter 2 originally appeared, in a shorter form, as "Conversion to the World View of Alcoholics Anonymous: A Refinement of Conversion Theory," *Qualitative Sociology* 6(1):5–27. Reprinted with permission.

Chapter 5 originally appeared, in a shorter form, as "Slipping and Sobriety: The Functions of Drinking in Alcoholics Anonymous." Reprinted by permission from *Journal of Studies on Alcohol*, Vol. 41, pp. 727–732, 1980. Copyright by Journal of Studies on Alcohol, Inc., Rutgers Center of Alcohol Studies, New Brunswick, NJ 08903.

BECOMING ALCOHOLIC

1

PERSPECTIVES ON ALCOHOLICS ANONYMOUS

F ROM THE THEORETICAL stance of symbolic interactionism, actors construct and respond to their worlds based on the meanings they develop with others through interactional processes. Different actors may construct and respond to the same phenomenon differently, and the same actors may change or use multiple meanings of the same phenomenon. Accordingly, there are multiple definitions of reality or multiple definitions of a situation. I came to know Alcoholics Anonymous (A.A.) from the perspective of a participant observer. However, I also came to know A.A. through empathizing with A.A. members and by reading A.A.'s literature as well as the social science literature on A.A. In this chapter, A.A. will be primarily discussed from the perspective of my experiences and that of A.A. literature.[1] My overall experience of coming to know A.A. might be called a data collection strategy, but somehow something is lost from that point of view (see Appendix A for a more typical and detailed statement of this study's methods). Participant observation allows the researcher to share in the life of the respondents and to see, feel, and appreciate the situations they encounter and the decisions they make (Becker, 1958; Bogdan and Taylor, 1975). The participant observer lacks the power as well as the desire to manipulate the setting. Rather, he or she tries to understand the setting from the actors' points of view without "going native" (Gold, 1958).

FIRST DAYS IN THE FIELD

Mideastern City A.A. staffs a service center where information and literature can be obtained and where persons can seek help twenty-four hours a day. I was cordially welcomed at the center and was given the names and locations of several meetings. The secretary in the center suggested that the weekly meeting of the middle group would be a good place to find out about A.A. in Mideastern City because it was well attended and because it drew many A.A. members from other groups. The first evening I went down to the middle group, I was scared. I arrived twenty minutes early and sat in my car, trying to convince myself that I wanted to spend a lot of time getting to know people who perhaps did not want to know me. Questions raced through my mind. How many people would be there? What if they would not talk to me? What if they asked me to leave? Would I know anybody there? What questions would they ask of me? Reluctantly, I left the car and headed for the modern church building in downtown Mideastern City.

Inside the glass doors were three separate hallways and a downward staircase. At the bottom of the stairs, a middle-aged male in casual clothes said that the A.A. meeting was upstairs tonight. When I entered the room upstairs, I was greeted by several hello's and smiles. Chairs were set up, and I noticed the friendly sound of a large perking coffee pot. Taking my coffee, I sat down close to a couple of guys who introduced themselves as Bill and Bob. At that moment, a woman walked over and asked me to read the Twelve Traditions at the beginning of the meeting. I hesitated and said, "My name is Dave, and I'm a sociologist interested in finding out about A.A. Am I allowed to read the traditions?" The woman, Beth, said, "I'm glad you are here and hope that you enjoy the meeting. I'll ask Bob to read the traditions." Bob and Bill made small talk with me about the university, the weather, and sports. As I spent more and more time in the field, I gained more and more acceptance and more confidence in myself, particularly in terms of coming to experience an organization from the participants' perspectives. Also, with time in the field, discussions gradually moved from the weather to advice and pleas for help, to personal problems, and to discussions about A.A.'s philosophy, literature, and success. In short, I moved from a tolerated intruder, an outsider, to a near-member. This transformation is significant because it allows the field researcher to share similar processes and experiences with members themselves.

Unlike other researchers (Lofland and Lejune, 1960), I did not try to pass as an alcoholic. Generally, disguised observation is unethical and it also lacks some of the advantages of adopting the "outsider" role (Trice, 1970). However, despite frequent statements defining myself as a researcher and denials of being "alcoholic," a minority of Mideastern City A.A. members came to view me as an "alcoholic" or at least "a latent alcoholic." This view, I think was a result of my heavy involvement in the field, along with the feeling by some members that I understood them. A.A. members believe that only an alcoholic can understand another alcoholic. A few members even questioned me about my drinking practices. The basic point of this is that I not only participated and observed the processes in which individuals came to regard themselves as alcoholic, but I also experienced some of these processes myself.

After that first day in the field, I spent sixteen months in and around A.A. groups in Mideastern City. Participant observation was conducted within a variety of A.A. settings, including the A.A. service center, open houses, open and closed meetings at various sites, and the homes and apartments of A.A. members. Each of these settings will be described later. Additionally, more in-depth data were collected from life-history interviews with a small number of A.A. members. Observation began during May of 1973 and ended during August of 1974.[2] The most frequently attended location was the weekly open meeting of the middle group. The middle group is the oldest group in Mideastern City and also one of the largest. Attendance ranges from twenty to sixty individuals each week. One distinct advantage of the middle group as far as data are concerned is the fact that it serves as a meeting place for members of many of the other groups in the area. As one member put it, "You can always go down to the middle group and find people you know from other groups just hanging around."

The role that I most emphasized within the field setting was that of a researcher interested in finding out about A.A. and about alcoholism. On occasion, a more complete description of this role was called for. To questions like "What are you trying to find out?" or "What is it that you specifically are interested in?" I replied: "I've read a lot of stuff about alcoholism. I've read what the physicians, psychiatrists, and sociologists think about it. Now I'm trying to find out what the people here think about it." Besides being an honest reply, this response nearly always received a favorable comment to the effect that anyone interested in finding out about alcoholism was welcome.

After five months of attending the open meeting of the middle group every week, I had established a good rapport with fifteen to twenty persons. However, some individuals merely said "hello" and nothing else; others did not seem to want to talk at all. Since several of the members I knew the best seemed to be influential in terms of their involvement and responsibilities, I decided to ask them (Abe and Ben) about the possibility of attending closed meetings. Closed meetings are for alcoholics only. I hoped that admission might enhance acceptance and further rapport and that data might be different in closed sessions. Ben responded positively but suggested that the next weekly closed meeting should be utilized, in part, to determine the members' feelings about admitting an outsider. The next week when I met Ben, the following exchange ensued:

> BEN: Everything is set for next week.
> DAVE (*Interviewer*): That's great. Thanks a lot.
> BEN: There were a couple of people who weren't too excited about your coming in, but I think the vote was thirty-nine to two.
> DAVE: I hope there weren't any hard feelings.
> BEN: No, there weren't. A lot of people stood up for you. Abe and I pointed out that we respected your honesty and integrity, that you were really interested, and that you had been coming to meetings for five months.

In retrospect, the most significant dimension of access to closed meetings was in terms of rapport.[3] The vote by the closed meeting on my admission brought me to the attention of virtually all the members of the middle group as well as members of other groups around Mideastern City. I received invitations to attend other meetings—both open and closed—and invitations to some of the more informal gatherings were also extended. These other acceptances further enhanced rapport by providing an opportunity to become better acquainted with some members and to talk at length about the program. On several occasions, I was quizzed by members about my knowledge of A.A. For example, one evening after a closed meeting at the suburban group, I was introduced to a member (Paul). After a few sentences of small talk, the following quiz took place:

> PAUL: I hear that you have been coming to meetings for over six months and that you are trying to find out about the program.
>
> DAVE: That's right. I'm trying to learn a lot.
>
> PAUL: What does the "first step" mean?
>
> DAVE: What do you think it means? (*My strategy in the field was to respond to questions by asking another question.*)
>
> PAUL: I know what it means; I'm asking you. (*With the tone of his voice, I was beginning to feel attacked. Nervously, I repeated the first step.*)
>
> DAVE: We admitted we were powerless over alcohol—that our lives had become unmanageable.
>
> PAUL: Well, you can say it; but what does it mean?
>
> DAVE: It means that people have to surrender. They must admit that alcohol controls their lives—that they are totally defeated.
>
> PAUL: How many times is God mentioned in the Twelve Steps?
>
> DAVE: Six.
>
> PAUL: Who is the higher power?
>
> DAVE: It's really up to the individual. It can be a traditionally defined God, a spirit, the group itself.
>
> PAUL: Good! (*I was hoping that he would start to back off.*) What does "one day at a time mean"?
>
> DAVE: It means that members should just focus on twenty-four hours at a time. It would be too difficult to think about not drinking forever. Instead, the goal is more reachable—a single day.
>
> PAUL: Okay, I guess. Have you read our literature?
>
> DAVE: I've seen the Big Book and a few pamphlets. If you have other stuff, I would like to read it.
>
> PAUL: I'll meet you at middle next week and bring you a couple of books. (*The following week, Paul brought sixteen books on A.A. or related topics and asked me to meet him ten days later to discuss them!*)

During these initial months in the field, I was quizzed five times. Later, during the study, I witnessed members quizzing newcomers and challenging them to get serious with the program. When newcomers successfully passed the quizzes, they got on with the program. When my responses to the quizzes were appropriate, I gained more acceptance. I began to be treated like an A.A. member. This became obvious when I was occasionally questioned during discussion meetings and when particular members asked me for advice and support. This point is significant because asking for support and advice and giving support and advice are the primary activities of group members. Generally, I tried to avoid giving advice as much as possible to reduce reactive effects. Sometimes, though, the situation demanded my comment or opinion.

By this time, six months of fieldwork had passed. As I gained more confidence and contacts, I began to attend different meetings, both open and closed. Additionally, more research time was spent at the open house because interaction there was constantly focused in small discussion groups; moreover, the conversations frequently had direct relevance to several of the research aims of this study. It was common for me to spend three or four hours at the open house after attending a meeting earlier in the evening. I became good friends with some Mideastern City A.A. members and became accepted as just another person by most of my A.A. acquaintances.[4]

The data in this study are drawn from these more personal settings and activities as well as from formal meetings and organizational activities. In fact, finding out how participants lived and defined their experiences outside A.A. became an early research focus. With that issue in mind, I conducted six life-history interviews at either the homes of A.A. members or my office. Each life-history subject was a male member[5] of A.A. with whom I had established rapport. In the selection of subjects, objective differences were maximized to obtain better results in terms of theory generation (Glaser and Strauss, 1967). For example, the perspectives of newcomers, old-timers, frequent attenders, working-class members, or upper-class members might provide different world views and give insight in terms of theoretical development. One particular feature of these interviews was the exploration of what Schur (1971) refers to as "retrospective interpretation." That is, what types of new explanations do members learn in A.A. to reinterpret their lives? Retrospective interpretations are no more or less true than current or future interpretations. They are simply different "vocabularies of motive" (Mills, 1940) or different interpretations of reality constructed to explain or to give meaning to a situation, setting, or experience. This point will be further elaborated in chapter 3.

A HISTORICAL SKETCH OF A.A.

Alcoholics Anonymous was developed by Bill W. and Dr. Bob, two alcoholics, in the late 1930s. The official beginning of A.A., as given in *Alcoholics Anonymous Comes of Age* (1957), is June 10, 1935.[6] However, the beginnings of the organization can be traced back to 1934, and the traditions out of which the organization evolved were dominant in American thought in the 1800s (Blumberg, 1977; Kurtz, 1979). According to Sagarin, the meeting between Bill W. and Dr. Bob "would not have led so easily to A.A.'s formation had there not already existed in America both the necessary social climate and a history of somewhat similar rehabilitative efforts" (1969, p. 32).

Early organizational forerunners of A.A. include the Washingtonian Society and the Oxford Groups. The former, a self-help movement for alcoholics, was popular around the 1850s. The basic thrust in the Washingtonian Society was for the alcoholic to serve as a model of successful renunciation and, in doing so, sell the Washingtonian program to others. McCarthy, commenting on this movement, reports that "everywhere the pattern was the same. A former inebriate, telling his story in dramatic fashion, was able to persuade hundreds in his audience to take the pledge and in turn become missionaries in the cause" (1958, p. 17). However, the organization ultimately became involved in political issues including abolition and temperance and, as a result, rapidly came to an end. At its peak, the Washingtonians reached a membership of somewhere between 150,000 and 250,000 (Sagarin 1969, p. 34).[7]

The Oxford Group was founded by a Lutheran minister, Frank Buckman, and it stressed that people could solve their problems by confessing their sins and dedicating their lives to God (Cantril, 1963). According to Bill W., the founder of A.A., "the early A.A. got its ideas of self-examination, acknowledgement of character defects, restitution for harm done, and working with others straight from the Oxford Groups and directly from Sam Shoemaker, their former leader in America, and from nowhere else" (A.A. *Comes of Age*, 1957, p. 39).

Bill W.'s personal struggle with his drinking spawned from conversations with an Oxford Group member and was aided by a "spiritual awakening." By following the principles of the Oxford Group and by trying to help other alcoholics with their drinking problems, Bill W. was able to maintain his sobriety. In May 1935, while on a business trip in Akron, Ohio, Bill had a desire to start drinking. Fighting off the temptation, he instead tried to seek out and help another alcoholic. Through Henrietta Siberling he met Dr. Bob, a local Akron physician (A.A. *Comes of Age*, 1957). Bill worked with Dr. Bob for several months, and Dr. Bob took his last drink on June 10, 1935. Since Dr. Bob was the first person Bill had been successful in getting sober, this date is given as the official beginning of A.A.[8]

During the next six years, A.A., led by Bill W., Dr. Bob and a few staunch followers, struggled onward. Primarily located in two pockets around Akron, Ohio, and New York City, the groups numbered around two hundred members. In 1937, A.A. groups began to separate from the Oxford Groups, and this separation was completed by the summer of 1939. During the same year, the book *Alcoholics Anonymous* was published. With its publication and with an article describing the success of A.A. in the *Saturday Evening Post* (Alexander, 1941), the organization experienced rapid growth and recognition. By 1957, several other books and various pamphlets had been published by the organization, and worldwide membership was estimated at over 200,000 (A.A. *Comes of Age*, 1957). Estimates in 1965 indicate that there were 12,040 chapters on six continents, and recent estimates by A.A.'s general service office in New York maintain that current membership is over one million (A.A. Fact File, 1984). Recent estimates and locations of A.A. groups can be found in Appendix B. Since A.A. keeps no official membership lists and since membership is determined by head count at local meetings, the above figures may be overestimates. However, there is no denying that A.A. is expanding. Acceptance of the A.A. program by the general public, alcohol professionals, and referral agencies, as well as an increasing belief in early treatment, are all factors indirectly indicating A.A. expansion. (Leach and Norris, 1977, provide a more detailed analysis of A.A. development and growth.)

The Organization Through Its Literature

Since Alcoholics Anonymous owns and staffs its own publishing company, there is a wealth of written material describing the activities of the organization. This literature is headed by *Alcoholics Anonymous* (1939, 1955, 1976), referred to by A.A. members as the "Big Book." This book serves as the basic text and manual for all A.A. members. Other books include *Alcoholics Anonymous Comes of Age* (1957), *The A.A. Way of Life* (1967), and *Twelve Steps and Twelve Traditions* (1953). Since 1944, A.A. has also published an international monthly journal, *The Grapevine*. In addition, A.A. presses have produced numerous pamphlets ranging from "Why A.A. is Anonymous" to "A.A. in Prisons" and "Student's Guide to A.A." Millions of these pamphlets are distributed yearly.

Briefly stated, A.A. is a self-help program run for and by alcoholics. A simple description of the organization appears on the first page of the *Grapevine* every month. According to the *Grapevine*,

> Alcoholics Anonymous is a fellowship of men and women who share their experience, strength and hope with each other that they may solve their common problem and help others to recover from alcoholism. The only requirement for membership is a desire to stop drinking. There are no dues or fees for A.A. membership; we are self-supporting through our own contributions. A.A. is not allied with any sect, denomination, politics, organization or institution; does not wish to engage in any controversy, neither endorses nor opposes any causes. Our primary purpose is to stay sober and help other alcoholics to achieve sobriety.

This description also appears in most other literature published by A.A. and is read at the start of nearly every A.A. meeting. Accordingly, it depicts the essentials of the A.A. program that its members wish to convey to outsiders as well as to newcomers. The essentials of the A.A. program are also represented by the twelve suggested steps of A.A. All A.A. members are strongly encouraged to use the "Twelve Steps" in dealing with their alcoholism and with life in general. The Twelve Steps as developed by Bill W. and some of the other founders are:

1. We admitted we were powerless over alcohol . . . that our lives had become unmanageable.
2. Came to believe that a Power greater than ourselves could restore us to sanity.
3. Made a decision to turn our will and our lives over to the care of God as we understood Him.
4. Made a searching and fearless moral inventory of ourselves.

5. Admitted to God, to ourselves, and to another human being the exact nature of our wrongs.
6. Were entirely ready to have God remove all these defects of character.
7. Humbly asked Him to remove our shortcomings.
8. Made a list of all persons we had harmed and became willing to make amends to them all.
9. Made direct amends to such people wherever possible, except when to do so would injure them or others.
10. Continued to take personal inventory and when we were wrong, promptly admitted it.
11. Sought through prayer and meditation to improve our conscious contact with God as we understood Him, praying only for knowledge of His will for us and the power to carry that out.
12. Having had a spiritual awakening as the result of these Steps, we tried to carry this message to alcoholics, and to practice these principles in all our affairs.

These steps make up a systematic model of the process of "becoming sober" as A.A. sees it, beginning with recognition of the fact that one has an "unmanageable life" and continuing through to the development of a commitment to "carry the message" to others. Of particular note is the fact that alcohol is mentioned only once, while God is mentioned quite frequently. In Mideastern City, A.A. members talk about and emphasize steps 1, 2, 3, 4, and 12 more than the others. Madsen (1974) reports that forty-one out of his sample of one hundred A.A. members had completed all of the Twelve Steps.

Members view the program as providing a specific model for arresting alcoholism, but they also see it as providing a general philosophy of life. Members frequently comment that "A.A. is a way of life," "A.A. is a philosophy of living," and "A.A. is a strategy of living that can work for anyone." A testimonial from a member, recorded in the "Big Book," states: "A.A. taught me how not to drink. And also on the 24 hour plan, it taught me how to live. . . . I am a part of A.A. which is a way of life. If I had not become an active alcoholic and joined A.A., I might never have found my own identity or become a part of anything" (Alcoholics Anonymous, 1955, p. 417). Individuals who successfully affiliate with A.A. have not merely found a technique which helps them stop drinking; they have also found a new lifestyle, a new perspective from which to view the world, and a new identity.

The only other codified set of principles involved in A.A. is the Twelve Traditions. These, again, were developed by Bill W. and some other influentials during the late 1940s and were adopted by the First International A.A. Convention in Cleveland in June of 1950. The Twelve Traditions "are a guide to better ways of working and living. And they are to group survival what A.A.'s Twelve Steps are to each member's sobriety and peace of mind. . . . The group must survive or the individual will not" (W. Bill, 1971, p. 1). The Twelve Traditions are as follows:

1. Our common welfare should come first, personal recovery depends upon A.A. unity.
2. For our group purpose there is but one ultimate authority . . . a loving God as He may express Himself in our group conscience. Our leaders are but trusted servants. . . . They do not govern.
3. The only requirement for A.A. membership is a desire to stop drinking.
4. Each group should be autonomous except in matters affecting other groups or A.A. as a whole.
5. Each group has but one primary purpose . . . to carry its message to the alcoholic who still suffers.
6. An A.A. group ought never endorse, finance, or lend the A.A. name to any related facility or outside enterprise, lest problems of money, property and prestige divert us from our primary purpose.
7. Every A.A. group ought to be fully self-supporting, declining outside contributions.
8. Alcoholics Anonymous should remain forever nonprofessional, but our service centers may employ special workers.
9. A.A., as such, ought never be organized; but we may create service boards or committees directly responsible to those they serve.
10. Alcoholics Anonymous has no opinion on outside issues; hence the A.A. name ought never be drawn into public controversy.
11. Our public relations policy is based on attraction rather than promotion; we need always maintain personal anonymity at the level of press, radio, and films.
12. Anonymity is the spiritual foundation of all our traditions, ever reminding us to place principles before personalities.

While the basic notions of individual treatment and of group survival are manifest in the Twelve Steps and Twelve Traditions, A.A.

literature provides additional information about definitions of alcoholism, symptoms of alcoholism and other related matters. According to A.A., alcoholism is a "progressive illness," (People and A.A., 1969, p. 7). The important question is not how much or how often a person drinks but, rather, what drinking has done to him or her ("A.A. for the Woman," 1968, p. 5).

A.A. also stresses the allergy conception of alcoholism (Trice and Roman, 1970b, *Alcoholics Anonymous*, 1955). According to the allergy conception, some individuals are physically more susceptible to becoming alcoholic than others. Alcoholism cannot be cured, only arrested, and the approach that A.A. suggests is permanent and continuous involvement in their program.

A.A. IN MIDEASTERN CITY

Alcoholics Anonymous was initiated in Mideastern City in March of 1949. However, a local newspaper reports that A.A. actually began in 1942 in a small community proximate to Mideastern City. The first group within the city proper, the middle group, began with two meetings a week: an open meeting for alcoholics and interested members of the public and a closed meeting for alcoholics only. By 1965, there were over twenty groups in the Mideastern City area, and meetings were being held every day of the week. By 1971, there were over forty A.A. sessions per week. At the time the data were collected, the meeting schedule for Mideastern City listed fifty-one separate groups holding seventy-two meetings per week in the city and the surrounding area. Since the average size of an A.A. group is twenty, there were approximately one thousand members in Mideastern City A.A. Currently, the Mideastern City service center estimates membership at over two thousand with over seventy separate groups.

Meetings represent the basic formal activity of A.A., in Mideastern City as well as in A.A. on the whole. Open meetings in Mideastern City are usually speaker meetings. Speaker meetings entail testimonials by members (usually two) who "tell their stories." Speakers most commonly define their role in terms of "telling what it was like when they were drinking," "explaining how they found out about A.A.," and "telling how good it is now." Members commonly refer to the drinking part of their story as a "drunkalogue" and to the "how

good it is now" segment of their story as the benefits of "sobriety."
Speaker meetings generally last one and one half hours, and if the
speakers are extremely short-winded, discussion may follow. Occasionally, in lieu of discussion, another speaker may be solicited on
the spot to tell his or her story in an impromptu fashion. At the
conclusion of speaker meetings, members band together in groups of
two to four and engage in conversation. Some of these groups discuss
the speaker's "message" but an equally typical focus is sociability.
Members find out "what's going on" and decide where they might
"hang out" for the remainder of the evening.

Closed meetings in Mideastern City are usually discussion meetings. They may be organized around one of the Twelve Steps. Since
the first step is regarded by many as the key to a firm foundation, it
serves as the basis for many discussion groups. Discussion groups are
also organized around topics that members might suggest. Closed
meetings that I attended have discussed loneliness, acceptance, anonymity, resentments, and sobriety. Lastly, discussion meetings
might address a particular problem that one of the members is currently having. These problems may range from family problems to
resentments, uncertainty about changing a job, depression, etc.
Closed meetings last around one and one half hours and frequently
a little longer. At their conclusion, informal discussion commences;
these discussions tend to be problem-centered, as opposed to the
characteristic sociability after speaker meetings.

Both speaker and discussion meetings are led by chairpersons.
Chairpersons are selected for short periods of time—usually a
month[10]—by a steering committee. The chairperson's responsibilities at a speaker meeting entail soliciting and introducing speakers,
reading the description of A.A. as found on page one of any *Grapevine*, asking two persons to read the Twelve Steps and Twelve Traditions, respectively, asking for announcements, and passing the basket
for donations. Chairpersons at discussion meetings have the same
responsibilities with the exception of obtaining and introducing
speakers. Naturally, chairpersons at discussion meetings are responsible for leading the discussion and making sure each member gets
his or her opportunity to speak.

The majority of the seventy-two weekly meetings in Mideastern
City are closed meetings (82 percent). Most meetings begin at 8:30
p.m. (56 percent). However, meetings are held every day in Mid-

eastern City at 9 a.m. and 12 noon, and several meetings are held
during the week after 11 p.m. With few exceptions, the meetings are
held in churches, schools, or in one of the three buildings that A.A.
maintains within the city—the service center and the two open
houses.

Attendance at most Mideastern City A.A. meetings averages
around twenty. Several discussion meetings I attended numbered as
low as four, while the monthly intergroup meeting held in a local
hotel averages sixty or more. Many members attend at least one
meeting per day and sometimes more. Meeting attendance is a constant topic and concern among most A.A. members, and it is common practice for members to inquire about a particular member's
whereabouts if he or she has not been seen in a couple of days. Most
members believe that not attending enough meetings is one of the
main reasons for losing sobriety. It is difficult to assess, however, how
many meetings are enough. For example, a 1961 A.A. pamphlet,
"A Clergyman Asks About Alcoholics Anonymous," reports that
"newcomers are encouraged to attend one or more meetings a week"
(p. 9). However, newcomers in Mideastern City are usually faced
with a challenge of "ninety meetings in ninety days." This usually
occurs after the newcomer has shown a degree of interest in the
program, as judged by some of the regular members. The most frequent estimate of minimal meeting attendance given by members is
three per week. This estimate varies upward more often than downward.

Mideastern City A.A. maintains a service center that operates as
the official link between A.A. and the community and functions as
the communications center for the seventy-one separate groups
within the area. Midday meetings are also held at the service center.
Additional functions include public relations, providing A.A. speakers for schools, and providing literature for the various A.A. groups
and other organizations that might need it. The service center is
staffed by a chairperson, a vice-chairperson, and a full-time secretary.

Another integral part of A.A. in Mideastern City revolves around
the "open houses." These two structures are large rooms furnished
with old couches, secondhand furniture, and utility tables. They
serve as places for members to come to during any part of the day for
conversation or relaxation. Besides informal conversation, the most
common activities at the open houses include chess, checkers, cards,
reading, and watching television. The busiest times at the open

houses occur between 10 and 11 p.m. nightly and on weekends. As previously mentioned, most A.A. meetings begin at 8:30 p.m. and adjourn around 10 p.m. Frequently, members attend open houses after their regular meetings are over. On weekends, members "hang around" the open house to "find out what's happening" and to meet their friends who cannot easily be seen during the week.

Open houses also serve as a convenient place for slippers (drinkers). The couches provide a comfortable place for them to "sleep it off," and the cupboard always has a healthy supply of honey to soothe their gastrointestinal organs. Prospective members also "wander" into the open house once in a while. Thus, open houses provide the main arena for confrontation between members and slippers and members and drinkers—a point to be elaborated further in chapter 5.

The older and larger open house serves brunch each Sunday morning, and since this gathering differs from the traditional A.A. meeting, some further comments are necessary. Sunday brunches are usually more relaxed than typical A.A. meetings. Wives and children are present, and the atmosphere is less serious and much more jovial than meetings or evening gatherings at the open house. From a functional perspective, the Sunday brunch might be characterized as "official time out" from the organizational regime of A.A.

Other more informal aspects of the organization have also been observed. These include picnics, dances, New Year's Eve parties, buffet dinners, and monthly fifty-fifty drawings to support the open houses. A.A.'s activities are so encompassing that the organization is best seen as a type of primary group. Most needs of the individual can be, and are, met within the confines of the organization. Medical and dental care may be provided by A.A. members. Automobiles may be purchased from salesmen who are group members. Meals, lodging, and transportation are also readily available upon request from any member. If persons need counseling or advice, they can seek it any time of the day or night from members. The frequency of this activity became obvious to me during interviews that I conducted at the homes and offices of A.A. members and also on other occasions when visiting A.A. members at their homes. Every time I visited, I witnessed phone calls from other members, who asked for advice, wanted to see how someone was doing, asked a favor, etc.

A high degree of intimacy and frequency of interaction is norma-

tively built into A.A. On numerous occasions, members commented that "after you are around the program for only a little while,
you find out that when somebody asks you to do something in the
program you do it." Doing something may mean "making coffee,"
going on a twelfth-step call, speaking, providing ride service, or
cleaning up after a meeting. Because of this high degree of involvement in terms of attending meetings, going on twelfth-step calls, and
in general spending most of one's time within the confines of the
organization, A.A. might be conceptualized as a greedy organization. According to Coser, greedy organizations "are not content with
claiming a segment of the energy of individuals but demand their
total allegiance." One of Coser's illustrations of a greedy organization, eighteenth-century American utopian communities, shows
considerable similarity with A.A. Coser argues that the utopian communities struggled for a "form of organization in which commitments would not be diverted from the one central purpose of fash-
ioning an ideal all-encompassing community" (1967, p. 208).

A.A. members have one central purpose: "to stay sober and help
other alcoholics to achieve sobriety" (*Grapevine*, 1974, p. 1). However, if this purpose is viewed in context, one observes that sobriety
can only be reached by members when they practice the Twelve
Steps and the Twelve Traditions, which encompass, in fact, a total
way of life or philosophy of living. Following this philosophy requires sacrificing one's individuality to the group, just as was the
practice in utopian communities. A.A. maintains that "personal recovery depends on A.A. unity" (from the first tradition). One A.A.
pamphlet, "The Twelve Traditions" (1971), argues that "our individual sobriety depends on the group. The group depends on us. We
soon learn that unless we curb our individual desires and ambitions,
we can damage the group." Member after member has stated in
conversations and speeches that "A.A. comes first. Everything else is
second. Nothing should interfere with A.A." Other members have
explicitly stated that "even our families have to stand back. They
have to realize that A.A. comes first because without it I would lose
my sobriety, and if I lose that I'm not any good to my family, am I?"

It may be that greedy organizations are necessary and more successful in gaining allegiance from their members and consequently
in promoting sobriety.[11] Gellman's study of A.A. (1964) reached similar conclusions when it compared A.A. to "total institutions" (Goff-

man, 1961). Organizations like A.A. are able to carry out their work more effectively when their members depend on them and no one else for the satisfaction of important needs. The greediness of A.A. is a type of commitment mechanism (Kanter, 1972) and serves to make members more involved in A.A. life and activities and less involved in outside life and activities (Robinson, 1979; Rudy and Greil, 1980). Greedy organizations act as social cocoons in their encapsulation of members from the outside world (Greil and Rudy, 1984) and thus may be effective in promoting sobriety and other identity changes.

2

THE PROCESS OF AFFILIATION WITH A.A.[1]

Since A.A. has a reputation[2] for being one of the best treatment approaches, if not the best, for alcoholism, the organization has been studied frequently by clinicians as well as social scientists. Several of the researchers have been particularly concerned with the factors that condition the process of affiliation with A.A. (Trice, 1957, 1959; Trice and Roman, 1970a; Leach and Norris, 1977; Boscarino, 1980).

In this chapter, data from A.A. testimonials, life-history interviews, and conversations with Mideastern City A.A. members will be used to describe the process of affiliation with A.A. My treatment of affiliation will emphasize the processes involved in becoming an A.A. member rather than the background characteristics of those who join A.A. In this chapter, I will frequently draw comparisons to the literature on religious conversion because religious conversion and acceptance of the A.A. ideology are similar processes (Gellman, 1964; Petrunik, 1972; Taylor, 1977; Chaiken, 1979; Kurtz, 1982). Travisano views conversion as "a radical reorganization of identity, meaning and life" (1970, p. 600). The philosophy of A.A. encourages one to define one's past experiences in a new way and to lead a particular kind of life—a type of life that is radically discontinuous with the past experiences of many A.A. members. The acceptance of different world views and life styles is the most significant element in what we view as conversion. Individuals who successfully affiliate with A.A. have not merely found a technique which helps them stop drinking; they have also found a new life style and philosophy, a new perspective from which to view the world, and a new identity.

BECOMING A MEMBER OF ALCOHOLICS ANONYMOUS

Most research on the "process" of affiliation with A.A. has not emphasized process at all but rather the psychological, physical, and/or social characteristics of prospective affiliates. Psychological characteristics which have been attributed to A.A. affiliates by various researchers include authoritarianism (Canter, 1966), ego strength (Seiden, 1960), extroversion (Edwards et al., 1967; Hurlburt et al., 1984), and "affiliative needs" (Hanfmann, 1951; Trice, 1959; Mindlin, 1964). Social characteristics purported to differentiate A.A. affiliates from nonaffiliates include: middle-class social status (McMahan, 1942; Mindlin, 1964; Trice and Wahl, 1958; Boscarino, 1980), small-group skills (Button, 1956; Trice, 1957), problem-sharing skills (Button, 1956; Trice, 1957), problem-sharing orientations (Trice, 1957), hospitalization for drinking problems (Bill C., 1965, Bailey and Leach, 1965; Edwards et al., 1967), and greater complications associated with drinking (Trice and Wahl, 1958; Edwards et al., 1967). In the most detailed affiliation study to date, Trice and Roman (1970a) explain affiliation by means of a combination of social traits, physical characteristics, and psychological predispositions. According to Trice and Roman, "the successful A.A. affiliate is characterized by affiliative and group dependency needs, a proneness to guilt, considerable experience with social processes which have labeled him as deviant, and relative physical stability at the time of entrance into treatment" (1970, p. 58).

All of the preceding research seeks to describe and explain affiliation as a consequence of the characteristics of the actor. The conclusions proceeding from this line of research have not, however, gone unchallenged. Many of these studies which have suggested that certain characteristics of the actor are important for affiliation have been contradicted by other studies. For example, although some researchers have suggested that A.A. affiliates are characterized by personality "health," Brown (1950) sees neurosis as a characteristic of A.A. members; Chambers (1953) and Jackson and Conner (1953) provide additional conflicting evidence. The data on A.A. affiliates may be characterized as an illustration in one organization of "Keller's Law," that is, "the investigation of any trait in alcoholics will show that they either have more or less of it" (1972, p. 1147).

Rather than focusing on the essential characteristics of A.A. affiliates or on *who* affiliates with A.A., we should focus on *how* one affiliates with A.A. In other words, a better understanding of the determinants of affiliation and of the nature of the affiliation process will be achieved through an actual examination of the affiliation process rather than through an attempt to find some magical characteristic which differentiates affiliates from nonaffiliates. Trice (1957) suggests the importance of examining the affiliation process when he points out the significance for affiliation of A.A.'s sponsoring system and the lack of competition with A.A. by the affiliates' significant others. According to Trice:

> The process begins before the problem drinker ever goes to a meeting. If, at this time, there is a self definition of sharing emotions and no willpower model in the background, if long time drinking friends are lost and there is exposure to favorable hearsay regarding the sincerity of A.A. members, a potential for affiliation has been produced.
>
> Upon first attending meetings, this potential is brought closer to fruition if the problem drinker has clear expectations concerning what meetings are like; if he is sponsored and the group exerts a positive effort to keep in close contact with him; if he has decided that the troubles of drinking outweigh the pleasures of drinking; and if he is not sensitive to social class symbols.
>
> The affiliation process is on the way to completion if, after attending meetings a few weeks, the problem drinker can readily adjust to the small, informal, spontaneous groups that develop before and after meetings, if his wife (or girl friend) does not compete with A.A., if his kindred have refused support in problems that arise form excessive drinking, and if he has been raised in a system of values that recognize the signs of having a drinking problem. (Trice, 1957, p. 53)

The intention in this chapter is to go further than Trice in emphasizing structural and situational factors as they relate to the process of affiliation to A.A. In contrast to Gellman (1964), Robinson (1979), Leach and Norris (1977), and Maxwell, 1984), attention will be paid to the processes that occur during the socialization of A.A. members. Leach and Norris view A.A. affiliation as following a process or phase model that includes:

1. Learning of the existence of A.A.
2. Perceiving A.A. as relevant to one's need.
3. Being referred to A.A. by a helping agency.
4. Making first personal contact with A.A., perhaps by telephone or by letter, but more likely face to face, involving (a) visiting an A.A. office, (b) visiting a clubhouse for A.A. members, (c) visiting, or being visited by, an individual A.A. member or two, or (d) attending an "open" (anyone welcome) A.A. meeting.
5. Attending a "closed" (for members or prospective members only) A.A. meeting.
6. Participating in various other A.A. activities, such as those related to the Twelve Steps and others which enable the alcoholic to internalize the norms of the movement, especially that of abstinence and those codified in the Twelve Traditions.
7. Taking the last drink.
8. Making a Twelfth Step visit (to help another alcoholic).
9. Speaking at an A.A. meeting, possibly resulting in disclosure to nonalcoholic acquaintances of one's A.A. membership. (Leach and Norris, 1977, pp. 483–84)

Although my model shares similarities with Leach and Norris, it differs in its focus upon process and situational factors in the shaping of affiliation or conversion. As I see it, the process of affiliation can be divided into six phases: hitting bottom, first stepping, making a commitment, accepting one's problem, telling one's story, and doing twelfth-step work. Before discussing each of these phases, I must emphasize that, collectively, these phases represent a "sensitizing" model for my data. There is considerable overlap in some of the phases. Some members complete twelfth-step calls before they tell their stories, and a few members never complete the latter steps. However, the model represents an abstracted version of the typical affiliation process in Mideastern City A.A.

HITTING BOTTOM

Most individuals who eventually affiliate with A.A. describe their initial contact with A.A. as a consequence of "hitting bottom." The phrase "hitting bottom" comes from the "Big Book," and it is used by A.A. members to describe the low point in their drinking careers, particularly when this low point meshes chronologically with their initial affiliation with A.A. Because the explanation that one comes to A.A. because one has "hit bottom" is ideologically prescribed, it is difficult to know the extent to which this explanation represents a conclusion drawn through a retrospective reinterpretation of one's alcoholic career rather than a description of actual life events. However this may be, it does seem logical that when persons become aware of a problem or are unhappy with their lives, they may seek out a perspective which offers a solution to their problem and a place where hope is offered that their situation might be changed for the better. Scholars of religious conversion talk about "hitting bottom" when they describe the importance of acute tension or personal difficulties in bringing and/or keeping affiliates involved in the process of conversion (Lofland, 1966; Lofland and Stark, 1965; Richardson et al., 1978, 1979; Richardson and Stewart, 1978).

"Hitting bottom" may refer to experiencing an intolerable amount of emotional pain, living on skid row, or finding oneself in some other tension-producing situation. It is typically associated with some sudden crisis which occurred as a direct or indirect result of drinking. The most typical crisis involves behavior that the drinker defines as unacceptable or intolerable. One speaker at an open meeting commented:

> Two terrible events forced me into this program. I had been supporting my drinking by rolling guys in the back streets of X city. One night I nailed this old guy and upon finding he only had eighty-six cents I vented my frustration by beating his head against the curb. I think I killed him. . . . A short time later my youngest daughter drowned and I was so drunk that I couldn't even go to the funeral. At this period in my life, things were so bad that I just had to do something, so I decided to come to A.A.

Maxwell's data provide a further illustration similar to my own example. "Two days before seeking help in A.A., I narrowly missed severely injuring or perhaps taking the life of my wife. I promised for the 1000th time not to drink again, yet came home drunk again. I then realized that I was powerless over alcohol and called for A.A. help" (Maxwell, 1954, p. 118).

These data illustrate that in the case of prospective affiliates of A.A., "hitting bottom" is a subjectively defined state. Members of A.A. discuss openly the fact that some people have higher or lower bottoms than others. One "hits bottom" when one believes that this has happened.

The subjective nature of "hitting bottom" is best conveyed through the following words of a chairman beginning an open meeting:

> Usually chairmen say a few words to qualify themselves, but if I started talking, we wouldn't have enough time. At any rate, I do qualify. Some people come in here because they lose a job or their wife, or maybe their home. It's usually for one of those reasons. Some people are forced to come here. I came on my own. I didn't lose much of anything. I wasn't forced into coming. I just knew I belonged here. Maybe I was a little different; I don't know. But the important thing to remember is that we are all alike once we get here because we gain sobriety. Besides that, it's a good philosophy. Like I said, I didn't lose that much, but I certainly didn't know how to live either. I'm positive on the way of life that this program has to offer. This program can really help anybody.

If "hitting bottom" is a subjective reality, the statement that one must "hit bottom" before one comes to A.A. does not explain any further why individuals make their initial contact with the organization. The question we should be asking is not whether or not "hitting bottom" precedes contact but how one recognizes that one has "hit bottom." My data suggest that this recognition was often "forced" upon the prospective A.A. affiliate by a significant other, a doctor, or an employer. The following dramatic account by a twenty-six-year-old male of a crisis event is a case in point.

> One night after a late drinking bout I got home and the door was locked. I pounded madly at the door and my wife came to the window with our two young children. She was crying and the kids were crying and she was saying, "You're a drunk, a drunk, a drunk—nothing but a drunk, a drunk. . . ." I also started to cry, at first I thought for the kids, but now I realize that I was crying for myself because it was the truth. I knew it was true and that I was a drunk. This incident really helped me

make the A.A. program; it was a moment of self-realization. Because of it, I went to A.A.

My field notes describe numerous crisis events that individuals define as central in leading them to approach A.A. The crises most frequently mentioned are the loss of a job or a spouse. On some occasions, even the threat of losing a job or a spouse is sufficient impetus to lead an alcoholic to try A.A.; indeed, spouses and employers use this threat as a power lever in pushing individuals to A.A. One respondent, who was married to an abstainer and whose career was conspicuously absent of unusual involvement with alcohol, commented that "my wife said she wouldn't talk to me as long as I kept drinking. She kept her word, and I just couldn't stand it, so I decided to do something about my drinking and go to A.A."

Robinson (1979, pp. 46–52) provides additional data that illustrate the influence and force of significant others—particularly family, A.A. members, physicians, and friends—in steering people toward A.A. Research by Jindra and Forslund (1978) supports this view by asserting that in Western City A.A. "most A.A. members are pressured into joining" (p. 118). Such pressures may explain Maxwell's view (1984) that A.A. is increasingly "attracting" more "high-bottom alcoholics."[4]

Life-history data from Dick, a thirty-year-old who has been in A.A. for six months, provide more specific detail about the process of hitting bottom:

DAVE: Because you were married and working long hours were you drinking substantially less at this time period?

DICK: No, I was drinking more; but the real problem was that sometime that year something happened: I just didn't seem to care anymore.

DAVE: Was that sudden?

DICK: When I look back at it, I would say it was gradual. You start letting things go. I had hobbies and interests and friends, and so forth. You stop seeing them, drop the hobbies, and your main interest becomes getting up in the morning, going to work, coming home, listening to the wife's bitching, and having a beer.

My wife and I were living in Iowa at this time, and I can remember in August of 1969 that she took the two kids and went to see her parents in Mideastern City. She was pregnant with our third child at that time. Anyway, she said that she was homesick. I had a lot of pressure from her and her parents to quit my job and move back to Mideastern City. After she was gone a few days, she called and said that she wasn't coming back. After a week or so, I went to Mideastern City to try and bring her back and I ended up staying. Did you ever feel totally defeated? I came here against my wishes, but I wanted to be with my family. We stayed with my in-laws until we found an apartment. I got a job and things were going okay.

Around Christmas, she and her father tried to force me to go to A.A. I went about twice a week just to keep them happy. I was working fourteen or fifteen hours a day and drinking on weekends. Then I lost my job and started drinking fairly heavily. We fought a lot about drinking and about money. I kept drinking on weekends, and instead of letting her know, I was buying pints of booze at bars and drinking them away from home.

Around here, my father got me a job in sales. I didn't like it but I kind of half-assed stuck with it. I was starting to drink a little more because there were more opportunities. It was during this time that my attitude began to change. I didn't give a damn. I felt as though I was forced here. I felt defeated. I did whatever they wanted me to do. If I didn't like it, I did a half-assed job.

My wife and I were always fighting. Every time she said something about my drinking or about my attitude it would start up. I would steam out of the house and deliberately not get drunk. That drove her bananas. She expected me to come home bombed and I didn't. Finally, I started to bring booze into the house because I didn't care what she thought anymore.

By this time, her parents had moved to California. There was a lot of heat on us to move out there, but I had played that game before. Last October, I came home from work, and there was a note on the refrigerator, saying that she and the kids had gone to California. They remained there until the middle of January, and it was in that period of time that I realized I had a drinking problem. I guess I knew I had a problem before but just didn't care about it. When she was gone, I had nothing to do. During this time, I was getting letters from the in-laws, telling me to sell everything—just get rid of the junk and move out here; but I wasn't about to do that. You get tired of running, chasing, or whatever. I knew if I moved out there, the whole thing would start over again. They would be running my life for me, or trying to; and I didn't want that. That was the thing that made me not care about things.

When she moved to California, I started drinking more heavily every day. I was drinking in the morning and drinking most of the day. During the evening, there was nothing to do, nobody to talk to, so I just watched TV and packed them away. You get to the point where you are either going to die or do something. After she had been gone for a while, I stopped drinking for two weeks. I decided to go to a psychiatric social worker and to A.A., but I went for myself—not because somebody was pushing me there. These two approaches [A.A. and psychiatric social work] had two different points of view. In A.A. the philosophy was that if you don't drink, you will get better. The social worker's big push was to find out why I was drinking. She delved into the past and came up with the conclusion that I wasn't an alcoholic. That set me on fire. I went out to a store and bought four six-packs and a pint. I drank the pint and one of the six-packs and passed out and blacked out. I was a perfectly normal drinker! Then, the next day, it dawned on me that if I were a perfectly normal drinker I wouldn't go out and buy that quantity of booze and drink it. So I went to A.A. again and I haven't had any problems since.

DAVE: Why did you go back to A.A.?

DICK: Well, like I said, things were really bad. With my wife gone and my being depressed, I guess I had reached the point where I wanted to kill myself. At least I thought about it. I never really tried. I guess something stopped it—lack of guts maybe. I think that these suicide thoughts were like a buzzer because I don't like pain, any pain, and killing myself didn't seem to have any future in it, to say the least. I had to do something so I went to A.A., and they said to hang around and things would get better.

FIRST STEPPING

The second phase of affiliation to A.A. is "first stepping."[5] "First stepping" entails making initial contact with A.A., picking up an A.A. guide, and becoming oriented to the A.A. program. Prospective affiliates approach A.A. in a variety of ways. Many individuals are made aware of the program through contacts with relatives and friends or through some institutional contact—prisons, mental institutions, hospitals, or detoxification programs. Many prospective affiliates call the local A.A. service center or one of the open houses to request personal assistance or ask for meeting information. Since the backbone of the A.A. program involves helping others as a means of maintaining one's own sobriety, members are always on the lookout for new recruits. However, assistance by members is seldom given directly unless it is requested. The prescribed procedure is for somebody to be close at hand when an individual is ready for help. A.A. works by "attraction" and not "promotion." The following excerpt from field notes illustrates the careful and supportive manner in which A.A. members try to get their message across. The excerpt also illustrates how tolerant A.A. members can be of drinkers even when there is little likelihood of immediately gaining a new member.

Friday Night at the Open House

I walked into the open house at 10:30 p.m., and there were ten people present, including two men in their early twenties whom I did not know. I sat down and started talking to Joe S. and Pat, and we talked about the newcomers.

DAVE: Joe, have you met or seen those two guys before?
JOE: No, not at all.
PAT: They came in earlier and are both in bad shape. The one talking to Bernie seems interested, but the other guy is really obnoxious.

As if on cue, the "other guy" stood up, pounded on the table and roared,

JIM: My name is James B. . . . and I'd like to say something. *(The reaction by everyone was forced tolerance of a loud drunk.)* My buddy Mitch and I have been having a good time down the street with some chicks and some booze. We just thought we would come in here and see what was going on. *(At this point, Joe S. started talking to Pat, and Jim exploded: "Shut up!")* I think you have a nice place here. You come around and shoot the breeze and don't drink and you like it. Well, I'm not ready for that stuff yet. Maybe someday, but not now. The way I figure it, I have a lot of fun left. *(Jim sat down.)*

JOE: Dave, when they come in like that there is nothing that you can really say.

DAVE: Yes, I guess he is in pretty rough shape.

JOE: He is nowhere near ready to listen to anyone.

JIM: Hey you, what's your name? *(This was directed to Joe.)*

JOE *(ignoring the question, comments in disgust):* That's what booze can do for you.

JIM: Hey you. I'm talking to you.

JOE: What do you want?

JIM: I just want to talk about drinking.

JOE: Why? Do you want to stop?

JIM: Me? Hell no! I don't want to stop. I like drinking and girls and fun.

JOE: You're so drunk you probably couldn't even get it up if a girl would look at you.

JIM: Bullshit! What would you know about girls anyway?

JOE *(ignoring the question):* Where did this guy come from, Pat?

PAT: He and his buddy were drinking at the Moose all day. His buddy looks like he might be interested, but this one is no-where near ready.

JIM: Hey, Joe, or whatever your name is. You think I'm drunk, don't you? Well you're right and I like it.

JOE: I used to like it too. So did everyone else around here, but we don't like it anymore.

JIM: Don't give me that bullshit. Why don't you come on down to Fred's and I'll buy you a drink.

JOE: I told you, we don't drink anymore. If you want to have a drink, go ahead.

JIM: Sure as shit I will. *(He staggers out the door.)*

PAT: The air is fresher now that he left.

DAVE: Do guys come in here like that very often? Has he ever been here before?

PAT: No, that usually doesn't happen. I don't think anybody has ever seen him before.

MITCH: Where did Jim go?

JOE: He went to have a drink.

MITCH: Where?

PAT: I'm not sure, I think down at Fred's.

MITCH: Well, Bernie, I'm not sure. I think I want to go have a beer. Maybe I'll see you again. *(Mitch leaves.)*

BERNIE: Sorry I didn't say hello earlier, Dave, I was into it with Mitch. I guess you could tell.

DAVE: Sure, nice to see you again. How is it going?

BERNIE: Pretty good, how are you?

DAVE: Real good. Did you ever see those two guys before?

BERNIE: No, never. They came in about an hour ago. The guy who was talking to me, Mitch, seems to be a little bit interested; but he isn't really ready yet. The other guy is nowhere near ready.

DAVE: What do you say to guys like that when they come in?

BERNIE: There isn't much you can say or do at all for guys like Jim. As far as Mitch was concerned, I just tried to be friendly and make him feel comfortable and accepted.

DAVE: How did he react?

BERNIE: Well, he seems pretty confused. I think the other guy is a bad influence on him. I just tried to make him feel a little less scared.

DAVE: Scared?

BERNIE: Sure, I can remember when I came in. I was really scared, and I'm sure Mitch was too. I gave Mitch my number and told him to call me any time. I also told him I'd be willing to take him to a meeting or at least meet him outside so that he wouldn't have to go in by himself.

DAVE: Do you think he might decide to come?

BERNIE: It's hard to say. I don't think he is ready yet, but when he is, he will find my number and call me. He asked a lot of questions about the program.

DAVE: What did he want to know?

BERNIE: Mostly things like what we do at meetings and questions about our views of alcoholism.

DAVE: How did you know he wasn't ready?

BERNIE: When you have been around for a while you can just sense it. He hasn't hurt enough yet. (*I never saw Mitch or Jim again.*)

When newcomers come to A.A., they are typically scared and confused and do not know what to expect. They have come into the program for a variety of reasons. Some have come on their own volition because they "have reached bottom and there is nowhere else to go"; others have come because they were pushed into the door by employers, friends, or wives. Some members come because they are "looking for a better way of life." Most people who show up at

A.A. meetings have problems with their drinking, but some people do show up who have other problems. Bohince and Orensteen's research (1950) in Minneapolis includes in this group "curiosity seekers," "nonalcoholic deviants," and "transients." In Mideastern City A.A., several members commented: "It really wasn't my drinking that brought me here. I just wasn't living right and I needed a new philosophy." Another member said he was a homosexual and was trying to figure himself out. Even many of those who do drink may not view themselves as "alcoholics" when they first encounter A.A. From the point of view of the prospective affiliate, the first task at hand is to discover what an alcoholic is and whether he or she is one.

The newcomer's first days around the program are usually spent attending orientation meetings or being personally oriented by an A.A. member. Orientation meetings generally revolve around a brief description of the disease nature of alcoholism as A.A. perceives it and a brief exploration of how the A.A. program works through its Twelve Steps and Twelve Traditions. Orientation meetings are often first-step meetings as well. That is, they involve discussion of the importance and meaning of the first step.

Newcomers are urged to attend A.A. meetings frequently, and they usually pick up a guide who will show them around various A.A. groups and the open houses. Typically, the guides are the individuals who first make contact with a newcomer, and they frequently become the newcomer's sponsor, if the newcomer affiliates and wants a sponsor. Guides are responsible for introducing newcomers to A.A. members, taking them to and from meetings, channeling them to the most appropriate meetings, and performing other similar tasks. Guides tend to be similar in basic characteristics to newcomers whenever possible. Through informal means, newcomers pick up guides of the same gender, age, and social class.

From the point of view of the organization, the chief function of initial A.A. orientation and guiding is to "qualify" the prospective affiliate, to get affiliates to recognize that they, in fact, do belong with A.A. The typical pattern here is to encourage newcomers to listen, in hopes that they can "identify" with guides or with other A.A. members. If newcomers express any interest, they are given a copy of the "Big Book" or some other A.A. literature.[6] As the title of this stage, "first stepping," suggests, the members try to move the newcomer to the realization that his or her life is unmanageable and that he or she is powerless over alcohol. It must be emphasized that virtually all who come are viewed as potentially qualified for the program. Specific comments that members have utilized to convince newcomers that they belong include the following:

> Any drinking can be a problem. All you have to do to be an alcoholic is drink.

> Only alcoholics come to these meetings. You have been coming to these meetings, and, therefore, you must be an alcoholic.

> If you want to stop drinking you can be a member. It doesn't matter if you drink a lot or not. All you have to do is desire to stop drinking.

> Some of us didn't drink much at all. It just seemed that when we did, we got into trouble.

> My feeling is that you have to ask yourself, "How does drinking mess up my life?" If drinking screws up your life and you do things that you wouldn't do if you weren't drinking, then you have a problem. And, if you have a problem, this program can help you if you work at it.

The newcomer is pressured to accept the label of alcoholic because A.A. members maintain that successful treatment is contingent upon realization and definition of one's problem. Chairpersons of A.A. meetings and A.A. testimonial speakers have made frequent comments before audiences in hopes of helping individuals qualify as "alcoholics." One comment made at a closed meeting particularly stands out: "If there are any new people here tonight, I hope that you learned something. If you think you have a problem or if you think you are an alcoholic, I assure you that you are. You wouldn't be thinking about it and you wouldn't be here if you weren't an alcoholic." Moderate drinkers, individuals with "problems in living," and the present author have been offered or have qualified for the "alcoholic" role.

During first stepping, members try to find out as much as possible about newcomers and provide them with a good deal of personal attention, support, and acceptance. The effort to deal with newcomers at a personal level frequently pays off. Newcomers have contacted A.A. uncertain about what A.A. is. Often they expect to find an

organization composed of "skid-row bums." In other words, they
expect the worst, and then they find it is not the worst. They are
often quite favorably impressed by the warm atmosphere they encounter at A.A. They are made to feel that they are among friends
and that A.A. members are the kind of people "who would do anything for you." Obviously, when newcomers are favorably impressed
with A.A., they are more likely to take on the A.A. culture (Maxwell, 1984).

A similar emphasis on intensive interaction and on the formation
of close personal ties within the group has often been noted in the
literature on religious conversion (Lofland and Stark, 1965; Lofland,
1966; Harder et al., 1972; Gerlach and Hine, 1968; Richardson et
al., 1978; Heirich, 1977). Lofland (1978) has recently described the
"hooking" techniques of a group whose success in prosyletization
seems to stem, at least in part, from the self-conscious manipulation
of a loving atmosphere. Various passages found in the "Big Book"
suggest that members of A.A. are also consciously aware that the
personal, informal, accepting approach may enhance their success
at recruiting new members.

> When you discover a prospect for Alcoholics Anonymous, find
> out all you can about him. (P. 90)

> Get an idea of his behavior, his problems, his background, the
> seriousness of his condition, and his religious leanings. (P. 90)

> Call on him when he is still jittery. He may be more receptive
> when depressed. (P. 90)

> See your man alone, if possible. . . . Tell him enough about
> your drinking habits, symptoms, and experiences to encourage
> him to speak of himself. (P. 91)

I suspect that the newcomers themselves are often aware of the role
that the personal approach plays in building up loyalties to A.A. One
sometimes sees at open meetings individuals who arrive after the
speaker has begun to talk and who leave as soon as the speech is over.
It is, of course, virtually impossible to contact these individuals in
order to discuss their motives for this behavior, but I suspect that the
pattern of coming late and leaving early may be a strategy consciously employed by individuals who wish to "check out" the organization without running the risk of "getting hooked." (See Straus,

1976, 1979, for descriptions of the conversion process that emphasize the tactics employed by seekers rather than those employed by
organizations and groups trying to attract converts.)

MAKING A COMMITMENT

During "first stepping," prospective converts encounter little pressure
to embrace the ideology of A.A. or to become active in the organization, but as soon as old-timers begin to think that an individual is
qualified for and genuinely interested in A.A., they begin exerting
pressure on that individual to "make a commitment." Pressure to
make a commitment is exerted at three levels: behavioral, ideological, and social.

The pressure to make a behavioral commitment to A.A. represents
an attempt on the part of the organization to provide prospective
affiliates with a sense of responsibility and purpose. Newcomers
might be asked to show up at meetings a little early, to set up chairs
for meetings, to empty ashtrays, or to help make coffee—not major
tasks, but performing them allows the newcomer to feel needed and
to experience a sense of contribution or responsibility. These responsibilities are usually given to those prospective members who need
them the most, that is, people who have lost most of their other
responsibilities and who have lost control of their lives—people with
low bottoms. Performance of such simple tasks may function as "side
bets" (Becker, 1960). Once prospective affiliates have invested some
time and energy in the daily operation of the organization, they have
more to lose if they decide not to affiliate with A.A. The more time
and energy are spent, the more will be seen as "wasted" should prospective affiliates decide not to "enlist."

Many organizations require new members to give up something
as the price of membership. Kanter (1972, p. 76) suggests that once
individuals have sacrificed something of value, they may be more
highly motivated to continue their involvement with a commune or
utopian community. Prospective affiliates of A.A. have not given the
organization all their worldly goods, but they have sacrificed some
time, and this may function in a similar way. Furthermore, for many
members, the "sunk costs" of behavioral commitment are directly
related to the rewards of sobriety. Mideastern City A.A. symbolically
rewards behavioral commitment and, most importantly, sobriety

through the presentation of various colored chips representing differing lengths of sobriety. The applause and praise following the awarding of "one month chips" provide newcomers with a tangible reward and yet another reason to continue coming to A.A. Individuals whose sobriety has now been publicly acknowledged and applauded may be unwilling to risk the humiliation that might come from "slipping" or from breaking off contact with the organization. When guides and members sense that newcomers are interested, they frequently ask them to "take the program seriously" by challenging them with the "ninety/ninety rule." In other words, they challenge newcomers to attend ninety meetings in ninety days. This behavioral as well as ideological commitment is viewed as a test of the newcomers' seriousness and also as a strategy to enhance the likelihood of sobriety and thus affiliation.

Lofland (1978) has used the term "encapsulation" to describe the process by which members of the Divine Percepts insure that prospective affiliates are unable to interact with any reference persons who might discredit the world view to which the prospective members are being exposed. In the case of the Divine Percepts, encapsulation is achieved primarily through physical segregation. Physical segregation as a means of preventing other world views, individuals, or groups from competing for the prospective converts' loyalties has been found to characterize other conversion situations as well as situations involving "brainwashing" and "deprogramming" (Harder et al., 1972; Schein, 1961; Lifton, 1963; Patrick and Dulack, 1976; Shupe et al., 1977). Affiliation with A.A., on the other hand, does not involve physical segregation from "the world." Prospective affiliates are usually not asked to give up their friends, their families, or their jobs, but the "ninety/ninety rule" serves as the functional equivalent to physical segregation. After all, persons who are going to ninety meetings in ninety days do not have much time to hang around with their drinking buddies.

The "ninety/ninety rule" minimizes the distraction to which prospective converts could be exposed from competing organizations or perspectives. In this regard, it is worthwhile to mention the function of A.A.'s satellite organizations, such as Alanon, an organization for close relatives of alcoholics.[7] Students of conversion have sometimes noted that proselytizing groups encourage prospective converts to sever or attenuate ties to significant others who are not involved in the group. A.A. usually employs a different strategy for insuring that the prospective convert is not subject to conflicting perspectives and demands for commitment. Instead of severing affective bonds with significant others, satellite organizations like Alanon function to unite the prospective affiliates' new reference group with previous reference groups by initiating the significant others into the A.A. world view.

At the ideological level, emphasis is directed toward the development of a commitment on the prospective affiliates' part to the organization's beliefs and values, specifically the Twelve Steps and the Twelve Traditions. Guides and other members begin to ask newcomers to study and know the program. Newcomers are expected to attend meetings and to work at "not taking the first drink a day at a time." They are invited and expected to "hang around" with members after meetings have ended and to go over to the open house for hours of informal discussion regarding A.A., its ideology, and its members.

Sometimes during the stage of "making a commitment," newcomers are challenged or quizzed about the program. Failure in these quizzes results in suggestions and demands to "get serious," "to be honest with yourself," and "to learn to work the program." It must be emphasized that little of the affiliation process described to date is formalized or highly structured. Most pressure for personal change occurs within the context of informal discussions. These discussions occur before and after meetings, at the open houses, and at members' homes; they involve detailed elaboration of members' experiences as active alcoholics and as active A.A. members. These experiences are always explained in terms of the Twelve Steps and the Twelve Traditions or in terms of other aspects of A.A. ideology.

With the immersion into behavioral and ideological commitment, social commitment ensues as well. Prospective affiliates begin to spend considerable time with their guides, sponsors, and other A. A. members, both within the confines of organizational activities as well as during "free time." One new member said: "They told me to avoid questionable persons, places, and things. The easiest way for me to do that is to hang around here (the open house) and to stay around A.A. people all the time." The functional consequence of social commitment as well as behavioral and ideological commitment is the encapsulation or separation of the prospective member from the outside world—the drinking world. A major identity change is easier to achieve if the change being sought (the A.A. view) is not under constant attack from alternative perspectives or from discrediting significant others (Trice, 1957).

ACCEPTING ONE'S PROBLEM

As individuals become more committed to the perspectives and activities of A.A., they are pressed to admit their "problem." This fourth phase in the affiliation process is highlighted by the prospective affiliate's acceptance of an alcoholic identity. In "first stepping," newcomers were qualified, but in accepting their problem, they verbally admit their alcoholism by saying, "My name is ——— and I'm an alcoholic." All members use this or a similar introduction before giving testimonials and before speaking at discussion meetings. Newcomers sometimes qualify their statements by saying that they think they might be an alcoholic or by saying that they are not sure. The public admission that one is alcoholic is quite difficult, and A.A. members press individuals to make this admission if they are reluctant to do so. I carried on the following discussion with a twenty-year-old male (Ted) who had been on the program for five months.

> DAVE: How long were you in the program before you admitted to yourself that you were an alcoholic?
> TED: That really bothered me at first. I think it took probably about nine weeks. I don't think I wanted to admit it because I knew the truth would set me free. The truth was all right for some people but not for me. It hurt.
> DAVE: What do you mean?
> TED: I think I was always hiding behind this phony self. I was always excused from whatever it was that I did wrong because it wasn't my fault. I think accepting my alcoholism was like accepting myself.

This respondent also described how acceptance of his alcoholism really helped him "work the program" and "gain his sobriety." Some A.A. members initially parrot the phrase "I am an alcoholic" and do not fully accept the identity until later in their A.A. careers. One forty-five-year-old male related: "I was simply parroting that I was an alcoholic until after about six weeks of going to A.A. I went out and got really drunk. Then I knew that I really was an alcoholic."

Once this identity transformation occurs, individuals are well on their way to affiliation. During this phase, the affiliate begins to work hard on the Twelve Steps, placing particular emphasis on making amends for past harms and on taking moral inventories. Inventory taking is completed by the affiliate himself (step 4) and later shared with a clergy person, another member, a close friend, or a relative (step 5). The most frequently mentioned character flaw discovered in inventory taking is resentment. Resentment "destroys more alcoholics than anything else. From it stem all forms of spiritual disease, for we have been not only mentally and physically ill, we have been spiritually sick. When the spiritual malady is overcome, we straighten out physically and mentally. In dealing with resentments, we set them on paper" (Alcoholics Anonymous, 1955, p. 64).

After self-appraisal, the affiliates are encouraged to share their shortcomings with God and with "another human being." In encouraging the prospective affiliate to share his or her inventory, A.A. is making use of a commitment mechanism which Kanter (1972, p. 103) has called "mortification." In mortification, individuals accept their subordination to the group and confirm their willingness to be judged according to the standards of the group. By acknowledging their character flaws in the presence of others, prospective affiliates demonstrate their ability and willingness to see themselves and judge themselves from the perspective of the A.A. ideology. Kurtz's history of A.A. (1979) emphasizes themes subsumed by mortification as the essential aspects behind A.A.

Another activity that occurs during this phase is the selection of a sponsor. Some members select sponsors at a later time, and a few A.A. members never select a sponsor, but that is clearly the exception. Sponsors become advisers in all matters around the program and in private matters as well. The selection of a sponsor is viewed as an important event, and the affiliate is not pushed into a choice. When members tell their stories at meetings, they frequently mention their sponsors by name and how they were responsible for helping them gain their sobriety.

TELLING ONE'S STORY

The affiliate's next step is to affirm publicly much of what has transpired in the past four stages. "Telling one's story" or "giving testimonial" is perhaps the best known aspect of A.A.'s organizational dynamics. Storytelling occurs formally at most open meetings and many closed meetings. It also frequently occurs piecemeal at discussion meetings and in informal conversations. The testimonial is made up of two parts: a story about how bad it was before A.A. and a story about how good it is now. A.A. members frequently refer to the drinking part of the testimonial as a "drunkalogue" and to the second part as a "sobriety story."

Students of conversion and commitment have sometimes pointed out the importance, for the commitment process, of a "commitment act" which symbolizes the initiate's incorporation into the group (Gerlach and Hine, 1968; Hine, 1970; Harrison, 1974; Toch, 1965; Wilson, 1978). Speaking in tongues or receiving the baptism of the holy spirit may serve for members of the Pentecostal movement as the "bridge-burning act" that separates their old identity from the new (Hine, 1970); in A.A., one acknowledges one's embracement of the alcoholic identity by telling one's story.

When newcomers first tell their stories, they receive considerable support from their friends and sponsors. In fact, these individuals first suggest when the newcomers should tell their stories, and they give help by suggesting what should be told and how it should be told. After telling their story for the first time, newcomers are warmly applauded and congratulated by their friends. There is no specific timetable for first story telling, but three or four months after initial contact is the earliest we have observed. Robinson (1979) reported that seventy percent of his sample of London A.A. members told their stories within six months. A few people rarely, if ever, tell their stories. An excerpt from field notes serves to illustrate the feel of the setting when "first stories are told."

Saturday Night at South Side

There were more people at the meeting that night—twenty men and thirteen women. Up toward the left front of the room, Don was seated at a table with four women whom I had never seen before. Later I found out that they were all from the town and country group and that one of them, Jackie, was going to tell her story for the first time. Jackie, about forty, was exceptionally well dressed in a black skirt, white satin blouse, black sweater, wrist bracelet, pearl necklace, and high heels. When Don introduced her, he commented that this was her "first time telling her story." As she left her seat, the woman next to her said, "Take it easy, you will do just fine." She began:

> My name is Jackie, and I'm an alcoholic. I'm glad to be here. I'm glad to be here for a number of reasons. First of all, I'm glad because perhaps I may be able to bring hope to one of you sitting out there. Perhaps I can share some of my experience, hope, and strength with some of you. The second reason that I'm glad to be here—grateful to be here—is that it is good for me. There are a couple of things that they suggest to you when you get in this program. Initially, they might include making coffee or just getting involved. Later, you are asked to share your message with others—that's what I'm doing tonight.

Toward the end of her story, she talked more about her initial contact with A.A. and about her first story telling.

> This initial acceptance that I was an alcoholic set me free, because I could accept myself and could accept the program. Everybody in the group was warm and friendly. I felt accepted and even loved. The initial step, the initial coming to A.A., is like getting off an elevator. A lot of people have told me this. The point is that you can get off the elevator at any floor and stop going down. Just like that, you can get off alcoholism at any point and you can stop going down. There isn't any reason that you have to go down all the way before you start back up. You can get off any time and stop it.
>
> It took me a while to really get into the program—to get the fog out of my head. The crucial point in making the program for me occurred when I realized that I needed everyone in the program. I needed everyone just to survive. My sponsor, Darlene, helped me tremendously. She helped me survive a divorce, and she helped me relate to my children. She is the reason that I'm here tonight, telling my story. She helped me so much I can never thank her enough. I love her. I thank and love all of you. I know I've been nervous, and my story may come across confused, but I know that you are behind me. I can feel the warmth of your feelings right now. Even though I haven't been in the program that long, I knew from the start that A.A. people are special people. This is a wonderful program. Thanks. *(The applause from the crowd was unbelievable. Jackie's friends stood up and welcomed her back to her seat.)*

After the meeting, five or six individuals came up and talked to Jackie.

RAY: You did a great job.
MAC: Thanks for sharing your story. You have a special message.
JACKIE: I was really nervous. The support from Darlene really helped me.
DARLENE: I knew you would do just fine. I knew you were ready.
FRED: Welcome to our group. I enjoyed your message.

Other "first stories" observed were similar to Jackie's in terms of the degree of group interest and support. Not only do testimonials represent a commitment act, they also provide a condensed version of the entire affiliation or conversion process. This version highlights the distinction between the "bad life" (drunkalogue) and the "good life" (the sobriety story). It contrasts the previous, unacceptable life style and identity with the newly found life style and identity and describes how anyone can make this transition.

DOING TWELFTH-STEP WORK

"Carrying the message" or doing "twelfth-step work" is the final phase of the affiliation or conversion process.[8] According to A.A. ideology, one is never cured. One can maintain one's sobriety only by remaining active in A.A. and by doing twelfth-step work. The importance of twelfth-step work, in this case in particular of a twelfth-step call, is illustrated by an exchange I had with Rick after an open meeting. He came in half an hour late, which was really unusual because he was always there early. He also looked shaken. After the meeting, I approached him, and we exchanged pleasantries until I joked, "You slid in a little late tonight—almost half time!"

RICK: I came from the hospital. I was on a twelfth-step call and it was pretty rough.
DAVE: How so?
RICK: Well, I knew the guy and his family, and he really was in rough shape. He's on the detox unit, and he has some really bad physical problems. I think what really shook me up was talking with his wife. I recalled some of the problems and havoc I caused for my family.

DAVE: Do you do a lot of twelfth-step calls?

RICK: Quite a few. I don't speak much and really I don't do a lot of the things that people do for the organization, so I do this. They help me a lot even if some are rough.

DAVE: What do you get out of them?

RICK: You realize that all the time you're only one drink away from going back to what you were. It reminds you, to say the least, and it helps keep you levelheaded. Sometimes, like to-night, it hurts, but it's the basis of the program—helping other people.

The "Big Book" offers numerous suggestions on the benefits of twelfth-step work for those who have gained their sobriety and on the most effective methods to employ in twelfth-step work. For example, it states that "helping others is the foundation stone of your recovery. A kindly act once in a while isn't enough. You have to act the Good Samaritan every day, if need be" (p. 97). Another suggestion is to "remind the prospect that his recovery is not dependent upon people. It is dependent upon his relationship with God. We have seen men get well, whose families have not returned at all. We have seen others slip when the family came back too soon" (pp. 97–98). Twelfth-step work also involves meeting all demands that might be encountered in spreading the word and strengthening the organiza-tion. Providing lodging and transportation, finding jobs, assisting in divorces—virtually everything is asked and expected of members.

Lofland and Stark (1965) have noted the importance of intensive interaction within the group if one is to become a "total convert." Through intensive interaction in organizational activities, converts maintain and renew their sense of commitment to the goals of the organization. By doing twelfth-step work, members of A.A. contin-ually act out their new self-conception. Through working for the organization, individuals have completed an identity transforma-tion. Their sense of self and sobriety has become contingent upon the organization's stability. This idea is recognized in A.A.'s "first tradition": "Our common welfare should come first; personal recov-ery depends upon A.A. unity." Much of what we have pointed out about "hitting bottom" and "first stepping" is relevant to doing twelfth-step work because the new member is now assisting other newcomers in their movement through these earlier phases. Mem-bers are expected to perform such acts whenever asked because twelfth-step work or helping other alcoholics is the most important dynamic within the A.A. program.

CONCLUSIONS AND IMPLICATIONS

The process of affiliation with A.A. includes hitting bottom, first stepping, making a commitment, accepting one's problem, telling one's story, and doing twelfth-step work. The affiliation process is structured in such a way as to enhance the likelihood that prospective affiliates will come to define themselves as "alcoholics" and make a commitment to "become sober." I believe that it also suggests an answer to the question of why some people who come into contact with A.A. stay on while others do not. The answer may be found not in differences in the characteristics of the affiliates and nonaffiliates, but rather in the different situations in which affiliates and nonaffiliates may have found themselves. Perhaps instead of asking ourselves "Do affiliates have greater ego strength?" or "Are affiliates more likely to come from the middle class?" we should ask such questions as "Are affiliates more likely to have been 'forced' into continuous contact with A.A. by reference others?"; "Are affiliates more likely to have reference others who support the goals and the perspective of A.A.?"; "Are affiliates more likely to have come into contact at A.A. meetings with individuals with whom they could identify?"; and so on.

Our description of the process of affiliation also illustrates that A.A., although it only asks that prospective affiliates "not drink, one day at a time," actually achieves a radical change in the affiliates' world view and identity through their acceptance of the A.A. philosophy and through their total absorption in the A.A. community and way of life. Identifying with A.A.'s view provides affiliates with explanations of their pasts, understandings of the present, and a basis for the future (Maxwell, 1984, p. 58). Such a radical reorganization of identity, meaning, and life (Travisano, 1970) is profitably viewed as conversion.

3

EXPLANATIONS AND THEIR FUNCTIONS

T HE PREVIOUS chapter developed
a general process model of affiliation with A.A. This chapter explores
a more specific question: What are the processes involved in the
designation of oneself as an alcoholic? How do A.A. members provide explanations or accounts of their alcoholism? This chapter will
emphasize the matrix of social interaction that A.A. members feel is
significant in their becoming alcoholic. While the focus is upon the
actors' selection, interpretation, and definition of events leading to
their becoming alcoholic, the most significant events result from the
interplay of the actors' behavior and meanings with those of the
various significant others involved in the total setting. Accordingly,
the unit of analysis is the interactional record or story of A.A. members. It must be emphasized that this information is overwhelmingly
a result of the actors' perception of their life events. Consequently,
the definitions of the situation are primarily the actors' definitions of
the situations and the actors' interpretations of definitions given by
others. This approach is similar to what current qualitative research-

ers view as phenomenology (Bogdan and Taylor, 1975) or reality reconstruction (Schwartz and Jacobs, 1979).

Members' explanations or accounts of their past activity and present behavior have been a popular sociological area of interest. Researchers have provided explanations from a wide range of individuals, including juvenile delinquents (Sykes and Matza, 1957), jurors (Garfinkel, 1967), suicide victims (Jacobs, 1967), child molesters (McCaghy, 1969), and "non-criminals" (Rogers, 1977). These studies view actors' explanations as indicative of the motives behind their actions in social settings. This chapter will describe and categorize the types of explanations that A.A. members in Mideastern City use in talking about their alcoholism, and it will discuss the consequences of these explanations for A.A. and its members.

When A.A. members provide explanations of their alcoholism, they are presenting what C. Wright Mills viewed as "vocabularies of motive" (1940). Such accounts represent explanations (motives) for one's behavior or for viewing oneself as an alcoholic that make sense to the actor and to others in the setting. In this manner, explanations are not retrospective interpretations of a person's alcoholism in the outside world or in any general setting, but they are explanations of a person's alcoholism within an A.A. setting, using "vocabularies of motive" learned and shared with other A.A. members. Similarly, in this view explanations (motives) are seen not as springs of action but rather as acceptable justifications that make sense out of a person's past and current life for the participants of a social setting.

Whether motives are viewed as situational or embedded, the point remains that "the differing reasons men give for their actions are not themselves without reason" (Mills, 1940, p. 444). The explanations presented in this chapter are derived primarily from testimonials delivered at open meetings. These testimonials depict many of the life events of one hundred A.A. members. Over one hundred and thirty testimonials were observed; however, several speakers related their stories twice, and a few members related their stories on three or four occasions.

TYPES OF EXPLANATIONS

Providing explanations of one's own and others' alcoholism is frequent among Mideastern City A.A. members, particularly during informal conversations, despite the fact that the "Big Book" argues that "to ask why is the wrong question." Newcomers are especially cautioned not to dwell upon "why" and to "get on with the program." A classic comment by one of Mideastern City's old-timers is: "It don't make any difference why you got it or how you got it. The important thing is that you got it, and A.A. will teach you how to handle it."

Despite these cautions, members, both new and old, constantly provide alcoholic explanations, which can be classified into two general types: disease explanations and moral explanations. Disease explanations are firmly grounded in A.A.'s belief that alcoholism is a spiritual, physical, and mental disease. Disease explanations explain one's behavior and one's alcoholism as a function of an allergy to alcohol, as *not* of the actor's making. Moral explanations reflect individuals' particular interpretations as they relate to becoming alcoholic. They suggest that a member's alcoholism was developed or exacerbated by character flaws.

Disease explanations are more frequently provided by members during the early phases of story telling and during the early phases of the taped life-history interviews. In both settings, the members are seeking to explain their behavior by providing a brief vocabulary of motive acceptable to the participants in the setting. Mills classically stated: "As a word, a motive tends to be one which is to the actor and to the other members of a situation, an unquestioned answer to questions concerning social and lingual conduct" (1940, p. 906). Disease explanations are acceptable in the setting because they support one of the most central tenets in the A.A. ideology—the idea that alcoholism is a progressive disease. Disease explanations are also prevalent during the informal conversations between members occurring after open A.A. meetings. Moral explanations, on the other hand, are most frequently noted near the termination of story telling and during informal conversations with other A.A. members, particularly at the open houses. During the later stages of story telling, some members begin to *ad lib* and express their personal opinions about themselves and their drinking through the use of moral explanations.

Disease Explanations and Their Functions

To say that individuals utilize disease explanations to account for their alcoholism is simple enough, but to explain how and why they come to adopt them is a more complex matter. Disease explanations are explanations gained through affiliation with A.A. that specifically represent the belief system of the organization. They are explanations that stress the disease nature of alcoholism or that stress that alcoholism is a response to a peculiar body chemistry. These ideas are represented in the "Big Book," the Twelve Steps, and various A.A. pamphlets. They are also represented in the rich oral tradition that pervades the organization. The most typical disease explanations that Mideastern City A.A. members utilize include the following:

> I became an alcoholic and I did those things because I was allergic to alcohol.

> I'm an alcoholic because I'm powerless over alcohol and my life had become unmanageable.

> I was born alcoholic.

> I really am an alcoholic but I didn't choose to become one. I became an alcoholic because I had an allergy to alcohol.

> I became an alcoholic because I lost spiritual, physical, and mental control of my life.

> I was doing things that I never would have thought of doing before. It was this alcoholic thinking that convinced me of my alcoholism.

Another detailed example from a testimonial of a thirty-five-year-old woman explains:

> Alcoholism is a spiritual, physical, and mental affliction. Those of us who have been in the program for a while know this from our experience. When I stopped drinking, I wasn't sober—just dry. In the beginning, I was drunk and I wasn't even drinking. So you see, alcoholism has to be more than just physical.
> Spiritually, my life was a huge void. I never prayed. In fact, I think I began to believe that there was no God and I didn't care about anybody or anything except booze. That's where the mental part comes in. Alcoholism is best understood as an obsession and a compulsion. . . . All of these factors—spiritual, physical, and mental—are part of being an alcoholic. This program taught me how not to drink a day at a time, and it taught me what alcoholism is.

The primary function of most disease explanations is that they release individuals from personal responsibility for becoming an alcoholic or, at least, severely diminish the responsibility. Diseases are generally not viewed as the fault of the persons affected; knowing that alcoholism is a disease allows the members to get on with the A.A. cure—not drinking for twenty-four hours at a time and being involved in the program. Acceptance of disease explanations does not require members to change their personality or drastically alter their way of thinking. All they have to do is terminate drinking.[1] Roman and Trice (1968) make a similar point when they interpret the allergy conception of alcoholism as facilitating sobriety in A.A.

Another function of disease explanations is that they provide a rationale to explain, understand, and account for many of the problematic behaviors that A.A. members may have emitted during their careers. In this case, they serve as a type of "account." Specifically, using the terms of Scott and Lyman (1968), they are excuse accounts in which members admit that their behavior was bad but deny full responsibility. Some of the behaviors that members account for with excuses include striking one's spouse, failing to provide financially for one's family, ignoring one's children, and cracking up the car. Illustrative of excuse accounts are statements such as "Alcohol caused me to do some bad things. I lost my job; I beat my wife; I screamed at my kids; and other things—some I don't even care to mention. But you must remember; it wasn't me who did them—it was alcohol." Or a second example:

I used to think that there was something seriously wrong with me, that I couldn't be only an alcoholic. I thought I was crazy or evil. I didn't know. A.A. helped me realize that my only problem was drinking. Alcohol was affecting my body, my mind, and my soul. It was like a cancer. The only thing wrong with me is that I can't drink. It was drinking that made me do all of those things, and it was alcoholic thinking that kept me from realizing it.

Disease explanations lessen personal responsibility, thereby making sobriety an easier task (one does not have to change one's self); additionally, they allow for excuse accounts of past problematic behaviors by utilizing vocabularies of motive acceptable to those in the setting. By lessening personal responsibility, disease explanations also

allow the significant others of A.A. members and outsiders to sus-
pend moral imputations regarding the alcoholic's drinking and to
lessen their own responsibility as well.

In addition to the functions that disease definitions provide for
A.A. members, they also have an obvious organizational impact. By
definition, disease explanations are organizational explanations of
the highest degree. They represent the sharing of the organization's
values among A.A. members themselves and between A.A. members and outsiders. When members utilize these explanations, they
affirm the organization itself. In essence, A.A. can best be understood as a systematic framework of explanations and/or norms pertaining to what alcoholism is, how one becomes afflicted, and how
one can make it back to sobriety and society. Trice and Roman (1970)
present a cogent argument by maintaining that the close relationship
between the A.A. perspective and middle-class American values explains, to a degree, the success of A.A. in the reintegration of alcoholics.

Moral Explanations and Their Functions

Moral explanations are more complex than disease explanations because they depict an individual's alcoholism as it evolved over a
number of years, in different environmental settings, and with several significant others, and because they reflect the individual's interpretation of alcoholism in his or her own words and not in the specific terms of organizational ideology. Yet more complex does not
necessarily mean more correct, more real, or more sociologically
interesting. Explanations, accounts, motives, and the like can not be
evaluated with "truth" claims. They come to be regarded as "true"
when they are accepted as such by participants in the setting. In this
sense, explanations can be viewed as the result of reality negotiation;
that is, through interaction or negotiation with other members and
themselves, members develop explanations that serve as appropriate
"vocabularies of motive" for the setting. The range of appropriateness
is influenced by A.A. ideology, as well as by the personal characteristics and beliefs of the member and his or her significant others.
Moral explanations, like disease explanations, are ideological in the
sense that they are learned and shaped within the organization. They
are also ideological because they are viewed as "character flaws" that

are important in the development of alcoholism from the organization's perspective.

An examination of field notes pertaining to testimonials and informal discussions, open house conversations, and coffee klatch reveals
a great diversity of moral explanations.[2] Most of these explanations
stress character defects. The most frequently occurring moral explanation is best characterized as the "big shot." Twenty individuals
specifically elaborated on this character trait and similar qualities like
"arrogance" as they influenced their drinking. Most of these individuals utilized this character trait as an explanation for initiating drinking as well as an explanation for continuing it. Illustrative of early
drinking explanations are the following:

> I guess I liked that bottle of beer. It made me feel like a big
> man.

> I used to like to have people talking about drinking. It made me
> feel big. It was great when my friends would ask if I had had
> my daily six-pack and I would say, "Shit yeah!"

> I always had to be top dog. I had to do bigger and better things,
> and for me that also meant I had to drink more.

> I always did wild things—even in grade school. I was a show-
> off and I had to get people to notice me. Because of that, I
> drank a great deal even back then (high school).

> I always did what I wanted to when I wanted to do it. I never
> listened to anyone. I knew all the answers and never wanted
> anyone's help. . . . I thought drinking was the smart thing to
> do. You weren't supposed to do it, so I thought it was good.

> I always had to be a big shot—a big man. Drinking big and
> spending money allowed me to impress my friends.

Once "big shots" start drinking, they tend to utilize similar reasons
in describing the continuance of their drinking. Comments illustrative of this include:

> I continued to drink and became an alcoholic because I liked
> to be a big man, and I could be anybody I wanted to be when I
> was drinking.

> I felt like a big man, hanging around in all those bars.

The best thing about drinking was that I could be a real big man. Sometimes I would tell other people in bars that I was a real big shot—a corporation executive, a manager, or something like that.

A second prevalent and closely related explanation (confirmed by seventeen members) revolves around the idea of "inferiority complex" or "not being accepted." While being a "big shot" involves searching for higher status levels, excelling, and utilizing alcohol to facilitate lying and bragging as well as fantasizing about one's status, drinking as a result of an "inferiority complex" can be viewed as allowing or facilitating social interaction or acceptance. The individual, in popular jargon, defines alcohol as a social crutch that provides him or her with acceptance. Examples of this type of explanation are:

I always had an inferiority complex and was withdrawn. Alcohol helped make me a little more active.

My hang-up was that I had an inferiority complex. I was a good student (graduated first in high school class), but I felt inferior. I started drinking in high school because I didn't fit in. I liked the effects of drinking because it made my inferiority complex go away.

My husband was older and was in show business. I felt inferior when I was with him and his friends, and drinking was the great equalizer. It made me feel better. After a few drinks, I knew I was just as good as anybody else. Drinking helped me socialize and get along with the crowd.

I don't even know exactly when I figured out I was an alcoholic, but I knew something was wrong with me even from the beginning. I didn't know what it was, but I knew something was wrong with me. Perhaps some of it was that I was never much of anything. I had all the opportunities but didn't use them.

I don't really know where to begin, but I can remember as a child that I always felt uncomfortable or dissatisfied. Even then I was unhappy with myself and later (at eighteen) when I started drinking, I think it helped me. That's why I became an alcoholic.

Some individuals are more specific than others about their perceived inadequacies, although they still fit the general theme of "acceptance" or "inferiority complex." For example, a twenty-seven-year-old male explained: "I wasn't a real happy kid. I was always quite a bit overweight, and when I began drinking at around sixteen, I began to like it right away. I liked what it did for me; it made me a different person." An older male (forty-five) gave a more sensational account of the "acceptance" theme, reminiscent of some of Goffman's comments about stigma (1963).

When I was five years old, my parents separated and put me in an orphanage. I developed, and still carry, to this day, a tremendous bitterness and resentment. I always felt unwanted and like I never fit in. I despised being an orphan. The first time I ever was accepted was in the Navy. I liked the guys; I liked the work; and I liked the drinking. When I was out drinking with the guys and got drunk, it was a great time. I think it was the first time in my life that I felt accepted.

A final account from a Mideastern City old-timer illustrates the theme of "acceptance":

When I was a real young kid, they found out that I had infantile paralysis. I spent quite a few months in the hospital, and a lot of people felt sorry for me. I always believed that despite my handicap I would make it. One leg was smaller than the other, but when I listened to my family or read *Ivanhoe*, I knew that somehow I was going to be a champion. When I was in grade school, I was quite good at a lot of athletics, but gradually the differences in my legs increased and it became more difficult for me to compete. However, I just knew that I really wanted to be good at something, and based on the stuff I had read, I thought I was going to make it; and I guess for my condition I was quite good, but I wasn't good enough to be great and that is what I wanted.

I didn't drink during adolescence because good athletes don't drink, but at eighteen I went to college. Lo and behold, I met the freshman football team, and this was really wonderful. As a 105-pounder, you know, I was their equal. They took me to a speak-easy, and it was the most wonderful thing that ever happened to me. There I was with these great big guys, and I was their equal. I could drink as much as any of them, and they listened to my opinions, so I joined part of this crowd because they drank. . . . I knew I was never going to be the world's champion football player, boxer, or handball player; but I could

be the world's champion drinker, couldn't I? Isn't that in all the
books, too, the gentleman who could drink for a long time and
then walk away? My friends only drank on the weekends, so I
found other friends that drank during the rest of the week as
well. Later in life, I lived and drank in New York's Bowery. I
drank with executives, with guys from the steel mills, and
with bean pickers. I could match all of them drink for drink
and even outdo them. . . . I could never be like some people
physically, but I was a champion drinker, and drinking made
me feel better.

A third moral explanation frequently mentioned (twenty individuals) in the field notes views drinking as a perceived solution to more
specific types of failures and frustrations—in popular jargon, as an
escape. For example, Ellen, the valedictorian of her high school
class, decided against attending college because of her involvement
with a boyfriend. When Ellen's boyfriend "dumped" her, she felt
doubly hurt and decided to use alcohol for relief. She commented
that "drinking made me feel better, and it helped to cover the hurt. I
couldn't have a good time without drinking." Other "frustration" type
explanations are illustrated by the following comments:

The only thing I got out of my marriage was four beautiful
children. My children were my life. When they were all in
school, I had a feeling of nothingness. I drank to relieve it.

When I was about fifteen, I began to notice that my parents
were fighting more and more. It was in connection with their
fighting that I discovered that drinking wine made me feel ob-
livious to their arguing. I thought that this experience of drinking wine and finding oblivion was the best thing in the world.
In fact, it created my own little world for me.

I really didn't like my job very much. Perhaps that is one of the
major problems that caused me to drink so much.

In addition to the general moral explanations already mentioned,
other explanations were noted but with less frequency. These explanations included: "drinking for maturity"; "going along with the
gang"; "drinking to feel grown up"; "drinking to get high." Only seven
members failed to offer a moral explanation for their alcoholism in
their testimonials.

Moral explanations, like disease explanations, serve as excuse accounts for one's untoward drinking behavior. More importantly, they are used for purposes of social differentiation in that they provide a sense of uniqueness for individual members. Members believe that alcoholic careers, while sharing many features, are also considerably unique. By developing the unusual features of their stories, they are sharing with the group new knowledge, and they are clearly offering assistance to members who might share these features. Many Mideastern City members have sponsors and A.A. friends who share similar moral explanations. Specifically, if a member's dominant personal explanations emphasize an inferiority complex, it becomes easy to get advice and support from a member with a similar "character flaw." Personal explanations also serve a social differentiation function in that some members are referred to by mentioning their first names along with comments about their drinking careers.

Moral explanations reaffirm the values of A.A., but they do so in a more general sense than disease explanations. Disease explanations specifically reaffirm A.A.'s notion of the allergy conception of alcoholism; moral explanations reaffirm the notion that A.A. members should take moral inventories and admit to others "the exact nature of their wrongs." Members are reminded of this obligation in steps four and five of the Twelve Steps. "Wrongs" are viewed in A.A. ideology and in oral tradition as "character flaws." Although not emphasized in A.A. ideology to the same extent as the disease model, they form an integral part of what Siegler et al. (1968) accurately view as the medical/moral model of alcoholism in A.A.

EXPLANATIONS AND BECOMING ALCOHOLIC

Explanations, both disease and moral, are related to an individual's becoming alcoholic in several ways. First, when individuals adopt A.A. perspectives by defining themselves as alcoholics and by explaining their alcoholism, they become secondary alcoholics (Lemert, 1951). Rather than using their alcoholism or a role associated with it to continue their behavior, they use it to cease their behavior. Secondly, after learning A.A. perspectives on alcoholic explanations, individuals become a particular type of alcoholic—an A.A. alcoholic. Through general processes of socialization, A.A. members come to highlight, reinterpret, and reconstruct their experiences and views regarding drinking and alcoholism.

Persons passing through different alcoholism programs come to
highlight different strategies, beliefs, and explanations regarding
their alcoholism. Some learn that their behavior is a consequence of
a disease and others that it is a habit. Some learn that they have an
allergy to alcohol, while others learn that they are orally fixated.
Accepting the views generally held by persons in a setting is a necessary condition for personal acceptance and progress in that setting.
A.A. alcoholics are influential in the processes by which others become alcoholics because A.A. members have provided the data for
the most widely accepted and utilized model of alcoholism—Jellinek's phase model (1946, 1952). A.A. and A.A. members are also
influential in that they represent the most powerful interest group in
the alcoholism treatment industry in the United States (Tournier,
1979). Accordingly, A.A. explanations and ideology are heavily utilized in the processing of alcoholics—a point to be discussed further
in chapter 6.

4

A TYPOLOGY OF CAREERS

Giving testimony or providing explanations for one's alcoholism illustrates that members are "acting out" dimensions of alcoholic roles as A.A. defines them. Most persons who adopt alcoholic roles within A.A. regard themselves essentially as alcoholics, and most are regarded as such by others both within and outside of the setting. Whether they are "real" alcoholics or not is a question that will be addressed seriously in later chapters. In acting out A.A. roles, in avowing deviance (Turner, 1972), members are required to reconstruct (Thune, 1977) their lives through the parameters of A.A. testimonials and A.A. inventory taking. As in the last chapter, my focus is on members' testimonials. However, rather than focusing on explanations, this chapter records broader themes illustrated by members in becoming alcoholic. In the coding of testimonials, two broad themes stand out because of their inclusion in nearly every testimonial. Specifically, nearly all members give testimony as to when they began to consider themselves as alcoholics (time of alcoholic self-definition) along with comments pertaining to their drinking in terms of what they drank, when they drank, how much they drank, and where they drank (drinking emphasis).

Brief illustrations of alcoholic self-definition include:

> I knew that drinking was causing me problems, but I felt that I could handle them. I guess after I lost my job, I began to think that I must have a serious problem. That's when I knew that I was an alcoholic.

> I must have been in the program for four or five months before I realized that I was an alcoholic.

> Back when I was living in Centerville, I read somewhere that drinking could be an addiction. It was then that I decided to quit drinking. After trying to quit a few times and not being able to, I began to wonder if I might have a problem. I came here and found out that I did

Some Mideastern City A.A. members provided even more detailed and graphic testimonials about how and when they regarded themselves as alcoholic, as well as illustrations of some of their drinking experiences. The analysis of these two themes was continued by treating each as a concept. The combination and dichotomization of the time of alcoholic self-definition and drinking emphasis yields the following four-celled property space:

		Time of Alcoholic Self-Definition	
		Before A.A.	After A.A.
Drinking	High		
Emphasis	Low		

Before the cells can be labeled, specific considerations of the operationalization of the two dimensions must be clearly stated. Operationalization of the self-definition dimension is straightforward. Field notes pertaining to testimonials and other relevant conversations were examined with respect to the time of self-definition as an alcoholic. Did the definition occur before the individual came to A.A. or after his or her A.A. involvement? The only problematic cases were individuals who made insufficient comments, who failed to pinpoint when they first considered themselves as alcoholics, or who contradicted themselves on this point. These difficulties excluded eighteen individuals from the base of one hundred A.A. members about whom detailed information was collected. One has no way of determining why these eighteen individuals did not provide information regarding the time of secondary alcoholism. Perhaps the information was merely omitted; perhaps the observer missed occasions when the information was discussed; or perhaps the individuals did not consider themselves alcoholics.[1]

The second dimension, drinking emphasis, is an indicator that subsumes several other dimensions. Drinking emphasis refers to the relative highlighting that A.A. members give to their drinking in talking about their careers. Drinking emphasis was measured by categorizing "sobriety stories" as low drinking emphasis and "drunkalogue stories" as high drinking emphasis. Stories that fit both categories were labeled according to the predominant theme. That is, if an individual's testimonial resulted in fourteen pages of field notes, and nine of the pages emphasized "sobriety" while the remaining five emphasized "drunkalogue," he or she was placed in the "sobriety" category and considered a low emphasis drinker. When individuals were well known outside of the context of testimonials, from personal conversations for example, the field notes describing these data sources were also utilized to determine the drinking emphasis dimension.[2] Only four individuals out of the base of one hundred provided insufficient information regarding their drinking or provided conflicting information that made it impossible to classify them on the drinking emphasis dimension. Of these four individuals, one also omitted information regarding the time of alcoholic self-conception. Accordingly, of the one hundred individuals, eighteen were excluded from the self-definition dimension and three additional persons from the drinking emphasis dimension for a total of twenty-one, thereby leaving seventy-nine individuals for analysis. Table 1 indicates the respective frequencies in each of the four cells of the property space.

Individuals falling in Cell A view themselves as alcoholic before attending A.A., and they emphasize their drinking activities highly. The label "pure alcoholic" will be utilized to refer to these individuals. Pure alcoholics are highly represented among what Jellinek (1952) referred to as "addictive alcoholics" and are similar to a stereotypical picture of serious alcoholics. Simply stated, this stereotypical conception sees alcoholics as extremely heavy drinkers who develop

Table 1. A Typology of Alcoholic Careers

| | Time of Alcoholic Self-Definition | |
	Before A.A.	After A.A.
High	Pure Alcoholic 24 (30%)	Convinced Alcoholic 34 (43%)
Drinking Emphasis	AB	
	CD	
Low	Tangential Alcoholic 8 (10%)	Converted Alcoholic 13 (17%)

social as well as physical problems as a result of drinking and who continue drinking partly to avoid alcohol withdrawal symptoms. Some A.A. members describe this type of alcoholic as "the guy who brings skid row home with him." Pure alcoholics have drinking careers ranging from four to twenty-four years (average of 11.4 years.), most are married, and all have histories of "problem" behaviors ranging from losing jobs, getting divorced, and being arrested for driving while intoxicated, to assaults, disturbing the peace, and breaking and entering. Pure alcoholics represent thirty percent (twenty-four individuals) of the individuals categorized in Table 1.

Field notes indicate that there are two different patterns involved in becoming a pure alcoholic. In the first pattern, the individual is convinced of his or her alcoholism by significant others or formal labeling agents and attends A.A. because of this conviction. In the second pattern, the individual, again with the help of significant others, approaches A.A. but rejects the program. However, the individual later comes back to A.A. as a secondary alcoholic. The initial rejection is usually due to the fact that the individual does not want to give up drinking or feels that perhaps he or she is not really an alcoholic.[3] These feelings are represented by statements like the following:

I couldn't relate to any of the things I heard, so how could I be an alcoholic.

I still had a job and everything was under control at home, so I didn't feel I was an alcoholic.

I guess I thought I had a little drinking problem, but I didn't think I was an alcoholic. I just didn't fit in.

When these individuals come back to A.A., they give the same type of account as the other pure alcoholics. The following are accounts illustrative of both patterns of pure alcoholics and also of accounts depicting the dramatic acceptance of an alcoholic self-definition:

My drinking was getting me in trouble. I knew I had a problem, but I didn't think I was an alcoholic. I lost the house, and I lost my job. Somehow my wife and my boss convinced me to go to a private setting and dry out. I attended a few A.A. meetings but still didn't believe I was an alcoholic. Then, one day, I just walked into a bar and started drinking. I didn't drink much, a few beers, and I got as drunk as I had ever been. Getting that drunk quickly made me realize that I really had a problem. I was defeated. I accepted my alcoholism and went back to A.A. and tried real hard.

I hadn't come out of the bedroom in days. It was just me and this bottle. The only thing I can remember is that on the fifth day my daughter came into my room and sat at the foot of my bed. I was thinking how beautiful she looked. She was thirteen, and her hair was long and straight and lying behind her head. She looked up at me and said, "Mommy, you are sick, aren't you?" I replied, "Yes Carol, I am sick. I have the Hong Kong flu." She said "Mommy, you don't have that." I replied, "Oh! Maybe it's the Asian flu." She said, "No, you don't have that. You have had that three times before." I replied, feeling guilty and thinking rather rapidly, "Oh, maybe it's a strep throat. There is a lot of that going around." She said, "Mommy, I think you are an alcoholic." I realized it was the truth. I realized that that was what I was. I realized that she was telling the truth and that I could never get myself to admit it before. But when she told me, I admitted it to myself for the first time, and I knew she was telling the truth. That wasn't all that Carol told me. She said, "Mommy, it's nothing to be ashamed of. It is a sickness. You are only sick—that's all." (*This individual went to A.A. within several days of this event.*)

Other accounts are less dramatic and less sudden in their self-concept effects.[4] One individual commented: "At this point in my life, everything was so bad I knew I had to stop drinking. I knew I was an alcoholic." Another indicated that from what he had heard and read about alcoholism, he decided that he had the problem and went to A.A.

In summary, pure alcoholics represent thirty percent of the A.A. members about whom I have detailed information. An outsider's guess would probably indicate that pure alcoholics represent the most frequent type of A.A. career. The data in Table 1 negate this common-sense hunch, and there is little reason to believe that Mid-eastern City A.A. is much different from A.A. in other cities in this respect.

Convinced alcoholics represent the most frequently appearing category in Table 1. Thirty-four members (43 percent) fit this category. Convinced alcoholics are individuals who regard themselves as alcoholics after attending A.A. They are "convinced" of their alcoholism because of A.A. ideology and because of the information they learn about the nature of alcoholism and about how it relates to their behavior. Convinced alcoholics, like pure alcoholics, typically evidence excessive drinking during their careers and give high emphasis to drinking in discussions and testimonials regarding their careers. Also, like pure alcoholics, they may approach A.A. on more than one occasion before affiliating. Convinced alcoholics do not regard themselves as alcoholics before attending A.A. They regard themselves as problem drinkers or as individuals having problems with drinking and thus are not secondary alcoholics.[5] Convinced alcoholics have relatively long drinking careers ranging from three years to thirty-nine years with a mean of 13.7 years. Three long careers (more than thirty-seven years) inflate this figure; and, again, it must be stressed that the cases are not randomly selected, are limited in number, and can only be construed in a "loose" variable sense.

Like pure alcoholics, most convinced alcoholics demonstrate problem behaviors across a wide spectrum. If there are no great differences on the problem dimension, why do convinced alcoholics lack a secondary deviant self-concept? There is no way of being certain, but a plausible interpretation is that the differences between pure and convinced alcoholics are a result of contingencies. Pure alcoholics may have more, or more powerful, significant others who convince them of their alcoholism before they attend A.A. Of course the opposite must be entertained as well—that convinced alcoholics are more successful in negotiating their deviance and hold off acceptance of the alcoholic role for a longer time.

A testimonial reflecting a convinced alcoholic career is expressed in the following example:

> I was playing the program, but I didn't think I was an alcoholic. I had been dry for a year. However, I was out of town one night, and there weren't any meetings to go to. I had dinner in a restaurant and managed to turn down cocktails. After dinner, just as I was leaving the restaurant, I stumbled into some people that I knew. I bought them drinks, but when they wanted to buy another round, I realized what was going to happen. I would either have to tell them I wanted ginger ale or take a drink. I ran out of the restaurant, and I was shaking and full of fear. At that moment, because of the compulsion, I admitted to myself that I was an alcoholic. The people at A.A. told me how the disease of alcoholism consisted of a mental obsession and a physical compulsion. Up to the time in the restaurant, I had never realized what the mental obsession was all about. Now that I had found out, I was convinced that I was an alcoholic.[6]

Another convinced alcoholic described his experience as follows:

> I've only been in the program seven months. I've been drinking, I guess, ever since I was about seventeen years old. In the last five years, though, my drinking has been a lot heavier. It has been pretty serious. I never had any problems though. I never got really sick. I never lost a job. The only thing that really bothered me was hangovers—sometimes. I didn't think I was an alcoholic and I'm not sure why I came to A.A., but it was after I got here that I got educated. I found out that my lack of all these problems (not getting sick and no blackouts) was a sure sign of my alcoholism. I listened and it made sense, and I admitted to myself that I was an alcoholic. I really enjoy the program here; this is a wonderful program.

Because convinced alcoholics represent the predominant pattern in Mideastern City A.A. and because they do not fit the stereotypical conception of an alcoholic, they raise some interesting considerations. How is it that individuals who do not consider themselves alcoholics can approach an organization that deals with the rehabilitation of alcoholics? As previously argued, one might answer—depending on one's theoretical and philosophical position—that convinced alcoholics are really alcoholics who are rationalizing. However, if one regards A.A. as similar to any other voluntary association, the answer might vary. When individuals approach voluntary associations, they are considering the possibility that the association might suit their needs and desires. Most individuals are not explicit about their personal needs or wants, nor are they certain that a particular association can fulfill them. Might not A.A. members be duplicating, in terms of typical patterns, what members and prospective members of other voluntary associations are doing?

Converted alcoholics differ from convinced alcoholics in that they do not emphasize drinking in their accounts. Converted alcoholics may come to A.A. with the belief that drinking is affecting part of their life, or they may come because significant others or legal officials force them to come; however, they come without alcoholic self-concepts.[7] Of the seventy-nine individuals in Table 1, thirteen (17 percent) fall into the converted alcoholic property space. Converted alcoholics[8] also differ from convinced alcoholics in that their acceptance of an alcoholic self-definition is characterized by more organizational pressure. With A.A., as well as with other treatment groups, there is a great deal of emphasis on problem definition. Admission of one's alcoholism is the first step toward recovery. It is difficult to remain within the group and manage to reject an alcoholic role. Because of this tremendous pressure to label and categorize, some individuals were convinced that I was an alcoholic.

While converted alcoholics experience many problems as a function of their drinking, their problems are less severe and usually limited to involvement with significant others. Other researchers have documented broad typing mechanisms within A.A. (Lofland, 1969) and other organizations (Freidson, 1966; Scheff, 1966). Regarding A.A., Lofland comments that

> anyone who displays even the slightest interest in the organization for almost any announced reason . . . is likely to be immediately coded as one who is seeking help, and A.A. members begin at once to impute to Actor the normality of his feelings and his power to change. Protestations by Actor that he has been misinterpreted are met with knowing, sympathetic smiles which acknowledge that the A.A. member is well aware of the difficulties of self-evaluation. (1969, p. 218)

One converted alcoholic, Harry, started drinking at seventeen or eighteen years of age. He married shortly after that, and his wife was a "teetotaler." He engaged in "fairly heavy" weekend drinking and argued frequently with his wife about his drinking. After a heated argument, she declared that she would not speak with him unless he stopped drinking permanently. Finally, Harry decided to look into the A.A. program. Harry remained in the program for several months before reaching the decision that he was an alcoholic. In his testimonial he said:

> For the next couple of months I was confused. I didn't know whether I should go to meetings or not. I didn't know if I had a problem or if I was an alcoholic. I'm not sure why, but I kept coming to meetings, and things got a little better with my wife. Finally, one night, I listened to a guy's story, and it was so much like my life that I could hardly believe it. I realized that I was a real phony. Now, I realize that I was an alcoholic all along. Everything that guy said that night was hitting me between the eyes. His story was like my life. I knew I had to be an alcoholic. I think everyone was relieved that I finally recognized that I was an alcoholic.

A second individual's account illustrative of converted alcoholism was presented to me in an informal two-hour conversation. Henry, the individual who related this account, was twenty-eight and a moderate drinker except on particular occasions. He drank more than his peers and ran into trouble as a result of his drinking. He was dropped from the state police training academy just prior to graduation because he was charged with public intoxication. His drinking also caused a great deal of conflict with his wife. She pressured him into A.A., and he "hung around," trying to find out if he had a problem. After three months and numerous conversations with many A.A. members, Henry developed an alcoholic self-conception. However, he had never spoken at a meeting and very infrequently said, "My name is Henry, and I am an alcoholic." Another A.A. member, who had been influential in introducing Henry to the A.A. program, told me that "Henry doesn't have much of a problem with drinking. He came from a well-to-do family and really his problems are with his wife. They are both immature and need some growing up to do."

Converted alcoholics differ from the traditional alcoholic stereotype even more than convinced alcoholics. Converted alcoholics are similar to Becker's "falsely accused" (1963). Again, the question arises, however, why a person would accept the alcoholic role if it is not accurate. First of all, the acceptance of this role might assist some individuals in solving their daily problems. Second, the alcoholic role as defined by A.A. is much broader than usually assumed, thus making acceptance easier. For example, Meyer (1969), an A.A. member, argues in his autobiography that any drinking can be alcoholic drinking. Even one beer a day could be alcoholic drinking, if a person needs that one beer. Third, there is a great deal of pressure to accept the alcoholic role. In chapter 6, evidence will be presented that virtually everyone who attends Mideastern City A.A. is offered, and offered very strongly, the alcoholic role, and when roles are defined and offered in settings where individuals frequently have little power, they typically are accepted (Scheff, 1966).

The last pattern describing A.A. members' alcoholic careers is the tangential alcoholic. Tangential alcoholics represent 10 percent (eight individuals) of the sample described in Table 1. Tangential alcoholics are characterized by a low emphasis on drinking plus an alcoholic self-conception prior to joining A.A. Tangential alcoholics are also characterized by a number of problem behaviors—some involving alcohol and some not involving alcohol. Some tangential alcoholics (six individuals) had experience with other official labeling agencies such as community health facilities, state hospitals for the mentally ill, and other psychiatric settings. The two other tangential alcoholics, although they had no formal labeling experiences, man- ifested behaviors that, if viewed by the appropriate audience, would have resulted in labels other than alcoholic.

The essential point is that tangential alcoholics explain their prob- lem behavior as a function of alcoholism and thus are alcoholics. If they and their significant others regard them as such, then sociolog- ically they qualify since we are utilizing a relativistic perspective. Furthermore, although tangential alcoholics manifest a pattern dif- ferent from those of the other three groups, it must be strongly em- phasized that they become alcoholics in very much the same way as the other alcoholic types. When individuals in any of the alcoholic career patterns regard themselves, and are regarded by others, as alcoholics and when individuals use these definitions to respond in an alcoholic role, they are alcoholics. That is to say that being alco- holic is a socially constructed categorization of behavior. Tangential alcoholics give testimonials that emphasize broad areas of concern in their lives. They frequently mention ideas such as "lack of love" in their lives and, correspondingly, "hating themselves and/or others" as typical of their problems of living. Accounts of tangential alcoholics have very little emphasis upon drinking. For example, Ester had a life characterized by a broken home, unwanted pregnancies, suicide attempts, and other problems. In her testimonial, she hardly ever mentioned drinking and related that "around 1970, I realized I had a problem. However, I didn't realize what the problem was. Looking back over my drinking experiences, I would say that I was incapable of love and that there was a tremendous lack of love in my life. Now I know I can really love people here in A.A., and the people here in A.A. are giving me love in return."

When Ester and other tangential alcoholics approach A.A., they believe that they are alcoholics. Whether this belief is a rationalization, a lie, or merely another definition of a complex reality remains to be seen. Whether one refers to Becker's typology and views tangential alcoholics as a special type crosscutting "secret deviants" and "falsely accused" or whether one views them as disavowing deviance (McCaghy, 1968) is a function of one's theoretical stance rather than objective reality. One individual representing this pattern stated: "My drinking isn't what really brought me here. I'm looking for a better way of life, a philosophy of living." Other A.A. members supported this statement by commenting that the individual involved had "mental problems" or was homosexual.

Another more dramatic example of the tangential alcoholic pattern is represented by the account of a thirty-year-old woman.

> People were following me; they were calling me names, and nobody was there. I used to hear people walking through my kitchen. One night when I was in the kitchen, I thought the walls were closing in on me. It was a very frightful experience. I didn't know if it was real or not. Everything was closing in on me. All of a sudden I looked up and out of the clear, like I could almost see it, something was telling me that I was an alcoholic. (*This individual initiated A.A. activity within three days.*)

One might challenge that in this account the individual may have been suffering from delusions and hallucinations as a function of alcohol. This may be the case, but it seems unlikely because of the low emphasis tangential alcoholics place on drinking.[9] The fact that tangential alcoholics represent the least frequent alcoholic career pattern might be due to an underrepresentation of this category of data rather than to a real difference. Specifically, tangential alcoholics might desire to withhold information regarding their careers and, accordingly, they may remain hidden. Additionally, it was difficult for me to question tangential alcoholics because of the moral consideration of "exposing another's cover" if they were hiding.[10]

Thus, the four general types of alcoholic careers are the pure alcoholic, the convinced alcoholic, the converted alcoholic, and the tangential alcoholic. Rather than viewing these careers as rigid categories or combinations of variables, one should see them as sensitizing concepts that represent a conceptual typology. This typology is a modest attempt to categorize most of the alcoholic careers of Mideastern City A.A. members. While few members have identical careers, most have enough similarity that they can be conceptualized into a general scheme. The scheme represents the culmination of a career or, more specifically, the culmination of a given phase of a career. This process might appropriately be called a phase of deviance avowal (Turner, 1972). A.A. and other social control agencies avow to virtually all comers a deviant role and/or a deviant identity. Likewise, many comers are actively seeking deviance avowal while others accept avowal under conditions of force or compliance. Acceptance of a deviant role can serve to reduce the ambiguities between "normal heavy drinker" roles and "problem heavy drinker" roles (Trice, 1956; Turner, 1972; Akers, 1977). Acceptance of a deviant role is rewarded by the avowing agency, and it may also be rewarded by one's significant others (Scheff, 1966, 1984; Lofland, 1969; Scott, 1969). Acceptance of the deviant role of the alcoholic may be more advantageous for some than the acceptance of other deviant roles, such as homosexual or mentally ill (Turner, 1972).

IMPLICATIONS OF THE TYPOLOGY

The typology of alcoholic career patterns developed in this chapter has implications for other deviant careers and for other typologies of deviance, particularly Becker's classic work (1963, 1973).

Table 2 presents a typology of processed deviance. Drinking emphasis is replaced with the label "problem emphasis" in that formal

Table 2. A Typology of Processed Deviance

	Time of Self-Definition as Deviant		
	Before Processing	After Processing	No Acceptance of Deviant Definition
High	Pure Deviant	Convinced Deviant	Intransigent Deviant
Problem Emphasis			
Low	Tangential Deviant	Converted Deviant	Falsely Accused

social control organizations, by definition, process individuals who have or who are believed to have some problem. "Problem emphasis" would be defined by the relationship between a person's behavior and the agency's criteria for processing. In a simple example from mental illness research (Scheff, 1966), the criteria for involuntary commitment were "danger to self and others" and "incapacitation." If a processed person fits these criteria, he or she has a high problem emphasis. If the person processed does not meet the criteria, he or she has a low problem emphasis. The column label in Table 2 is "time of self-definition as deviant" and not specifically alcoholic. Additionally, the label is trichotomized and not dichotomized because a third logical possibility exists—that of not accepting the definition of oneself as deviant. This possibility was excluded in Table 1 because no cases were included within the property space.

This typology of processed deviance deals with deviance that is processed by any social control organization, while Becker's typology deals with processed (pure deviance and falsely accused) and nonprocessed deviance (secret or potential deviance). Becker's typology deals with the processing (defining) of deviance at a general level, including what Schur (1971) views as the interpersonal, organizational, and collective rule-making levels, while the typology of processed deviance deals with the interpersonal and organizational levels. Because of these similarities, the career patterns developed in my typology can be utilized to elaborate the processed deviance within Becker's typology. However, it must be noted that the major typological dimensions in my study, while related, are not exactly the same as Becker's, so I am taking some liberty in this comparison.

The categories of pure deviance, convinced deviance, and intransigent deviance are subtypes of Becker's pure deviance. Pure deviants have committed the action in question and have labeled themselves and/or have been labeled by others prior to affiliation. Convinced deviants are the same as pure deviants with the exception that they do not view themselves as deviants until during or after their affiliation or processing, that is, until after they are "convinced." Intransigent deviants, although fitting the problem definition in question, refuse to accept the designation of themselves as deviant. Intransigent deviants would more likely be found in programs where admission is less voluntary than it is in A.A.

The categories of tangential deviant, converted deviant, and falsely accused are all subtypes of Becker's "bum rap" or falsely accused. Individuals placed in these categories do not fit the criteria of the processing agency very well, if at all. For some organizations, establishing processing criteria would become exceptionally difficult. For example, in A.A., on the official level "the only requirement for membership is a desire to stop drinking." However, as I have discussed under "first stepping" and as I will discuss again in chapter 6, individuals are specifically qualified by using typing questionnaires and through comparisons with other members.

This typology of processed deviance can be applied to the study of the rate production process within all social control agencies. It could be utilized profitably as a sensitizing concept to be further developed with empirical verifications of studies in agency affiliation and socialization. Different agencies processing the same types of problems could be studied to determine their effectiveness or lack of it in terms of problem definition. Agencies with higher percentages (determined empirically) in the bottom-row cells might be regarded as "problem-hunting" agencies, while agencies with higher percentages in the top-row cells might be designated "problem-solving" agencies, at least in the sense that they select persons who have the "problem" in question. Scheff's research (1966) illustrates that a state mental health facility has more patients that fail to meet the processing criteria than patients that do. Accordingly, such a facility would be viewed as a "problem-hunting" agency. However, the specific degree of "problem hunting" could only be developed in a comparative context. Research could also be focused upon how individuals specifically became typed and/or typed themselves into these categories. Additionally, the impact of the categories on an individual's success or lack of success within a treatment or rehabilitative setting could be explored. Finally, the typology could be applied to any setting in which people are processed. Voluntary associations, corporations, the military, and educational settings could all be examined by utilizing the patterns developed in the typology of processed deviance.

5

SLIPPING AND SOBRIETY[1]

S LIPPING" is the term that A.A.
members use to describe their own or another member's drinking.
Observations at open houses and informal discussions with A.A.
members indicate that slipping is a common occurrence within Mideastern City A.A. In this chapter, I will illustrate the dynamics and
importance of slipping within A.A. as contributing to both group
and individual success. Additionally, slipping will be viewed in a
broader theoretical framework within the sociology of deviance.
While the focus in prior chapters has been on members' accounts,
this chapter highlights interaction among members and between
members and "slippers."

THE FREQUENCY OF SLIPPING

Slipping is directly counter to the A.A. mandate of "staying sober a
day at a time." Accordingly, it qualifies as a serious norm violation.
Gellman's ethnography of A.A. (1964) viewed only one behavior as

more serious than slipping—"attacking the A.A. program." Slipping
is a frequent occurrence in Mideastern City A.A. During thirty-eight
visits to one of Mideastern City's open houses, I witnessed slippers or
observed slippers confessing to A.A. members or the group on eighteen occasions. In addition, on thirty-four of the thirty-eight visits, I
observed and/or participated in discussions regarding members who
had recently slipped or who were still in the process of slipping.

Other researchers using more quantitative strategies have specifically illustrated the frequency of slipping. In a study of London A.A.
groups, Edwards et al. (1966) pointed out that 57 percent of their
respondents had slipped at least once, and 18 percent had slipped
five or more times (1966, p. 383). These findings lead Edwards to
suggest that "the number of times members have 'slipped' since joining A.A. serves to emphasize that A.A. is as much a society of alcoholics who are having difficulty in remaining sober as it is one in
which they are staying off drink" (1966, p. 383). In a study of North
American A.A. groups, the A.A. general service board reported in
1970 that 41 percent of the A.A. respondents had not had a drink
since first attending A.A. By implication, then, 59 percent had
slipped at least once. Bailey and Leach (1965) and Edwards et al.
(1967) present data that indicate that twice as many respondents reported a year or less of sobriety as reported a year or less of A.A.
membership. Other studies (Smith, 1941; Bohince and Orensteen,
1950; Bill C., 1965; Jindra and Forslund, 1978; Polich et al., 1980a;
Ogborne and Bornet, 1982) document the frequency of slipping, but
because of methodological problems, the rates cannot be meaning-
fully interpreted. However, the implication of these studies is clear:
slipping is a normal and frequent activity.[2] The classic question of
functional sociology remains: "What are the functions of slipping for
Alcoholics Anonymous?" The following observations suggest that
A.A. groups create pressures and provide expectations that encourage slipping (deviance) and that the function of that deviance is
boundary maintenance.

SLIPPING AS A REAFFIRMATION OF NORMS

Since Durkheim's studies (1938), sociologists have been aware of the
normalcy and the functions of crime and deviance within human
groups. Crime is "an integral part of all healthy societies" (Durk-

heim, 1938, p. 67), and its primary function is that of boundary maintenance (Erikson, 1966). Commenting on his work and on Durkheim, Erikson states:

> The deviant act, then, creates a sense of mutuality among the people of a community by supplying a focus for group feeling. Like a war, a flood, or some other emergency, deviance makes people more alert to the interests they share in common and draws attention to those values which constitute the "collective conscience" of the community. Unless the rhythm of group life is punctuated by occasional movements of deviant behavior, presumably, social organization would be impossible.[3] (1966, p. 4)

The "collective conscience" and group boundaries are reaffirmed because deviance draws people together and encourages them to dichotomize deviant behavior and normal behavior. However, not only the norms that are involved in the violation are reaffirmed. For example, when a delinquent is apprehended for stealing a motor vehicle, not only the norms regarding theft and honesty are reaffirmed but also the assumed causes of the behavior as they are reflected in other norms. The person who stole the car may have violated curfew, may have been "hanging out" at a pool hall, or may have been truant from school. Violations such as theft then reaffirm norms regarding honesty and private property, as well as all the norms associated with the assumed causes of the theft. Accordingly, in A.A., when someone slips, the norms that are reaffirmed include sobriety and slipping as well as the other norm violations involved in leading the person to slip. Therefore, our discussion of slipping must also entail the other norms involved with slipping.

A.A. members frequently mention circumstances and behaviors that must be avoided in order to keep from slipping. These include depression, jealousy, overtiredness, an affair, or an argument with friends, or they have to do with not paying attention around the program, not practicing the program, criticizing the program, being dishonest, being too concerned with finances or other problems, being too happy or cocky, getting low grades or failing when high grades or success are expected, recalling old drinking memories, failing to avoid questionable persons, places, or things, and not attending enough meetings.[4] The following statements, taken from discussions among members at open houses, are characteristic of the comments that members use to disseminate information about these circumstances and behaviors.

> The mental part of this thing [alcoholism] can creep up on you when you get tired, and if it does, the next thing you know you will be drinking.

> We must always be careful of self-pity. One minute you might be feeling sorry for yourself and the next minute you will be slipping.

> If you don't keep active in the program, you will problem slip.

> As soon as you think you've got this program made and are feeling pretty good, you will probably slip.

Mideastern City A.A. members are constantly told by other members to avoid these circumstances lest they slip. The range of items is so encompassing, the normative structure is so highly specified and articulated, that one would expect many norm violators and therefore many slippers. The earlier documentation clearly indicates that slipping is a common occurrence. However, neither my data nor anyone else's cited explain slipping rates. The point remains that at the *normative* level, A.A. members believe that these norm violations frequently lead to slipping and that once norm violation occurs, slipping can be avoided by seeking reinforcement from the group. It is extremely important to note that in either case (that is, norm violation followed by slipping or norm violation followed by group support), the boundaries of the group are strengthened and reaffirmed.

Frequently, when members who have slipped return to a group for the first time, there is discussion of the circumstances of their slipping. Such discussion reflects A.A.'s emphasis on "being honest with yourself." During this type of discussion, other members find out what circumstances engender slipping and what they should avoid doing. Illustrative of these processes are the following statements:

> When I saw him making eyes at her, I knew they were headed for trouble. (*This situation depicts an affair; both members subsequently slipped.*)

> I'm not sure how it happened. I was feeling real good. I thought I had this program made. The next thing you know I was drinking.

Just take a look at me. Take a good look. If you take a drink,
you will end up just like me. At least I'm here though—that's
what's important.

A more detailed confession occurred at the open house one night.
In the middle of a closed meeting, Bernie surprised a number of
people as he stood up and said:

My name is Bernie, and I'm an alcoholic. I'm glad to be here
because I have to tell you something. Today I went out to Marcell. Some friends I hadn't seen in a long time invited me out,
so I decided to go. While I was there, they offered me a drink.
I thought about it for an instant, but I took it. Yes, Bernie took
that drink. Bernie did it. He didn't have to, but Bernie did.
Maybe Bernie shouldn't have gone to Marcell. Maybe he
should have known that old friends would ask him to have a
drink. Maybe, Bernie should have said no, but Bernie didn't.
He took that drink, and Bernie knew what would happen. How
many times has Bernie gone home and has had his woman
smell it on his breath and say, "get out." Maybe I should just go
home and pack my suitcase now and spend the night at the
Jackson Hotel.
    I didn't have to come here tonight and tell you, but I did.
Because if I didn't, the only one I would be hurting is Bernie.
Yes, Bernie is the one who drank, not you, but Bernie. Don't
feel sorry for me. If it were you, I wouldn't feel sorry for you.
Bernie doesn't even feel sorry for Bernie. He is just being honest. I'm not apologizing, I'm just telling you, so that I can be
honest with myself. Because, you see, Bernie *needs* this program, Bernie *needs* all of this, but Bernie threw it away by
drinking. How many times will I do this? I've done it before. I
can remember being down in the gutter and praying to God. I
said, "Please God, please take away all the pain and give Bernie
one last chance." How many more chances will Bernie get? I've
had them before. I guess Bernie isn't grateful. I knew that all
this would happen, but I still took that drink. Yes, Bernie took
it, and now he has to pay for it. Thank you. I'm sorry.

During "confessions" of this sort it is obvious that members involved
are learning about the events and circumstances that they must avoid
in order to keep from slipping. Since slipping or not slipping deter-
mines membership in A.A.,[5] the members, when involved in slipping discussions, are reaffirming group boundaries.

If an individual fights slipping by coming to the group for support, boundaries are still reaffirmed, as can be seen in the following excerpts:

> Sue was depressed. It seems that she may get a C in her course, and she usually gets A's and B's. I think she will be all right since we talked about it.

> My financial situation had been pretty bad for a long time, but I was thinking about it yesterday, and the whole thing began to snowball. I began to feel worse and worse, but it's OK now. At least I'm here.

> My daughter had on this old record. I began to think of those days when I was drinking and hanging around bars and doing a lot of partying. I turned it off and came right to the meeting. I told you about it and got it off my chest.

Since the above quotes represent flirts with danger (slipping), their discussion among members represents additional evidence of the boundary maintenance function of deviance in groups. Not only all the slipping norms are reaffirmed but, more importantly, also the norms involved prior to slipping and the norm of seeking group support.

I have argued that A.A., by creating a normative structure that is almost impossible to follow, creates deviance. This deviance is then used by members to reaffirm and strengthen the boundaries of the group. This finding is not surprising, for sociologists have frequently emphasized that deviance is likely to appear at those points where it is most severely proscribed in the normative order. Erikson states:

> Every human community has its own special set of boundaries, its own unique identity, and so we may presume that every community also has its own characteristic style of deviant behavior. Societies which place a high premium on ownership of property, for example, are likely to experience a greater volume of theft than those which do not, while societies which emphasize political orthodoxy are apt to discover and punish more sedition than their less touchy neighbors. (1966, pp. 19–20)

The contention still remains that although the argument has been built upon observation, some of the inferences, particularly in terms of A.A.'s encouragement of deviance, have been mine. However,

A.A. members are aware that slipping has beneficial aspects, particularly in terms of reminding them "what it was like" and in allowing them to help slippers, thereby building upon their own sobriety. The following statements are illustrative of the importance of observing and helping slippers:

> It does a lot for me to see what drinking can do for you. (*At this point the respondent points to a slipper sleeping it off on the couch in the open house.*) I can remember when I was like that.

> ROY (*a slipper*): When did you have your last drink, Fred?
> FRED: Right now, you just had it for me.

> Every time I confront a slipper it reminds me of what I was like and what I can be like if I don't follow the program perfectly. If you ask me, helping slippers is what makes the program tick.

These sample statements represent the members' awareness that their sobriety is dependent upon interaction with slippers. This awareness of the necessity of slipping indicates that slipping and the responses it generates are significant in boundary maintenance and, by implication, in group solidarity.[6] Additionally, slipping points out to the drinker and to abstinent members the vulnerability that each must face daily if he or she is to remain an "arrested alcoholic." From members' own perspectives, slipping is the dynamic mechanism that makes A.A. work in that it continually reminds them of their vulnerability and focuses constant attention in the A.A. arena on the normative structure that promotes individual sobriety. A.A.'s response to slippers generally is characterized by tolerance and assistance (Alcoholics Anonymous, 1955; Gellman, 1964). This response along with the members' discussion of slipping incidents allows for a near-constant flow of prescriptions and proscriptions associated with slipping in particular and with the A.A. program in general. It allows the group to develop and share its information concerning drinking behavior with slippers and other members, and, according to Clancy (1964), it allows sober members to participate vicariously in the experiences of slippers.

> "Slips," or short periods of drinking while endeavoring to adhere to abstinence and the A.A. program, are recognized and given tolerance by other A.A. members and are recognized as unfor-

tunate. Indirectly, however, slips do have a value both to the drinking and abstaining members. The A.A. member who slips quickly finds that his drinking is again to excess, that he disappoints others, and instantly opens many old sores. His experience serves to convince him again of the need for abstinence. His fellow members, through identification, receive the same dividends. In this manner reinforcement of the need for abstinence is propagated through the group. (1964, p. 517)

In broader sociological terms, slipping is a normal feature of the group, and the response to slipping strengthens group boundaries.[7]

Excerpts from a closed meeting at the open house provide graphic detail of the argument developed in this chapter. In the excerpt, a pair of slippers (Bob and Mary) arrive at the open house. Bob and Mary walked in with another man whom I did not know. Mary was in rough shape—stumbling and whimpering. Bob had also been drinking but did not appear as wobbly as Mary.

MARY: I want everybody to know that I have been drinking. I'm sorry. I didn't mean to. It just happened. I haven't had a drink for a long time and I love this program and I'm sorry.
RUTH: It's okay Mary. At least you are here. It will be all right now.
MARY: I'm scared. Why did I do it? I've ruined everything. I hope I don't just keep on drinking. (*She was verging on hysteria.*)

At this point, Mary sat down alone on one of the couches and began to whimper. Bob sat at the end of the table and, placing his elbows on the table, rested his head in his hands. He remained silent for most of the evening. Clair began talking with Mary, and four of us engaged in a discussion of Joe's future job plans. At a quarter to midnight, Joe said:

JOE: There is a meeting at midnight. Why don't you stick around?
DAVE: Well, I don't want to impose on anybody. I know it's a closed meeting, and other people may rather keep it closed.
JOE: Don't worry about it, Dave. Ruth, you're chairing tonight, aren't you?
RUTH: That's right Joe.
JOE: Do you think it would be all right for Dave to stay?

Ruth: I don't have any objections. I guess it would be okay.
Dave: Are you sure? I don't want to cause any hard feelings.
Joe: Look, it's all right.

At this point, Ruth opened the meeting. She mentioned that an outsider was present—and asked if anyone had any objections. No one did. After reading the Twelve Steps and Twelve Traditions, Ruth commented:

> Since Mary and Bob are here and since they had a lot of trouble, let's have a first-step meeting. (*"First step meetings" discuss the first step, particularly the aspects of being "powerless over alcohol" and having an "unmanageable life."*) My name is Ruth, and I am powerless over alcohol. That's why I don't drink anymore. I didn't want to be an alcoholic, but for some reason I am. I can remember how bad it was, but it's much better now. I can also remember slipping once that I thought I had the program made. So you see, Mary, that we all slip sometimes. The important thing is that we are both here now. Eddie, do you have anything to share with us tonight?
>
> Eddie: My name is Eddie, and I'm an alcoholic. I drank too much and too often. I lost my children and my family, so you can see my life was unmanageable. As a matter of fact, it was unmanageable for a long time, at least until I came into the program. Mary, I'm glad you are here. You too, Bob.
>
> Bob: It's good to be here. This time I'll make it work. I'm not sure about her [Mary].
>
> Mary: I'm glad to be here, too. It sure beats drinking in that bar. Why did I ever do that? I hope I can stop.
>
> Eddie: You have to stop, Mary. To drink is to die. If you go on a drunk, it may be your last one. Just remember, you have a disease and to drink is to die. That's all I have to say, except that I'm glad I'm here and that this is a wonderful program.
>
> Ruth: Fred, would you like to say something?
>
> Fred: No, not really. My name is Fred, and I'm an alcoholic. I'll pass tonight.
>
> Ruth: Joe?
>
> Joe: My name is Joe, and I'm an alcoholic. My life was getting more and more unmanageable all of the time. I didn't know what was going on. Finally, I just knew that the program would help me, so I came in. Things have been getting better ever since, but it's real slow.

RUTH: Would you like to say something, Bob or Mary?

BOB: I'm glad I'm here, and I know I can make it work this time.

MARY: All I can say is I didn't mean to drink. (*She was crying, very loud and hysterical.*) I don't know what I did. I ruined everything.

A few other members spoke and some passed. Ruth closed the meeting, and Eddie walked over and sat down next to me.

EDDIE: Dave, have you noticed the self-pity in Mary? That will really get you. It's all downhill after that.

DAVE: You mean that she will continue to drink?

EDDIE: I'd bet on it. Once you start feeling sorry for yourself, you're in trouble. I bet she starts drinking again tonight.

DAVE: Is there any way to stop her?

EDDIE: Probably not, and besides she has got to want to stop herself. If she doesn't, then there is no use trying to help her.

DAVE: What should she do to help herself?

EDDIE: Well, she should stop feeling so sorry and stop talking so much and do some listening and hang around the program more. Hanging around bars and not going to enough meetings will always make you slip.

DAVE: Do a lot of people have trouble slipping?

EDDIE: I slipped a couple of weeks ago.

DAVE: How did that happen?

EDDIE: Well, I was kind of depressed. I didn't have a job, and I was walking by this bar. I guess I shouldn't have been doing that, but I was. Anyway, I just decided to go and have a beer. I only had one, but I bought a six-pack and took it home. The next day, I felt bad about it and I called a friend in the program. He said not to worry about it and that I should get to a meeting.

DAVE: Well, at least you're back now and it's going okay.

These notes illustrate how members use other members' slipping to assist their own sobriety. The slippers remind them of their own vulnerability and provide them with a reason to discuss the first step of A.A.'s program—a step that A.A. members believe is the most important in the program. Such discussions also reaffirm the normative structure of the organization—a structure that leads to slipping as well as sobriety.

6

THE CONSTRUCTION OF ALCOHOLISM:
A.A. AND JELLINEK'S PHASE MODEL

I̲N THE PREVIOUS chapters, I described and analyzed basic processes related to the A.A. program and its members. Members' accounts and testimonials and field notes describing action within A.A. provided the basic data in the analysis. As far as members' accounts were taken as data and explanations in their own right, the analysis could be considered phenomenological. However, in the interpretation of affiliation and slipping, the analysis became more sociological. Sociological views of "conversion" and "deviance" were used to illuminate action within A.A. from a sociological perspective.

This and the following two chapters will be cast in broader terms. As this section unfolds, more and more emphasis will be directed toward the relationship between A.A. ideology and the reality of alcoholism in contemporary America and the relationship between the ways in which Mideastern City A.A. members think about alcoholism and the ways in which alcohologists think about alcoholism. The development of this theme begins with an analysis of the most widely influential model of alcoholism on the contemporary scene, Jellinek's phase model, and the impact of A.A. ideology upon it. This will be followed, in chapter 7, by a broader theoretical critique of the disease model of alcoholism and the development of a sociological definition of alcoholism. The final chapter will develop further how much of the contemporary sociological literature on alcoholism can be cast in terms of A.A. members' beliefs. Although the views of A.A. members will be utilized in the following pages, they will increasingly be bolstered with references to recent literature on alcoholism.

JELLINEK'S MODEL

Jellinek's phase model of alcoholism (1946, 1952, 1962) "has been the standard textbook description of the alcoholism process. It has essentially gone unchallenged until recently" (Albrecht, 1973, p. 19). Jellinek's model and his other writings on alcoholism, specifically *The Disease Concept of Alcoholism* (1960), have highly influenced most conceptualizations of alcoholism and its treatment within the past several decades (Lender, 1979; Heather and Robertson, 1981). The phase model reflects Jellinek's assessment and interpretation of data collected by the *Grapevine*, the official organ of A.A. The initial study (1946) was based on ninety-eight usable questionnaires from a "sample" of more than sixteen hundred A.A. members. The later presentations (1952, 1962) represent data collected between 1946 and 1952 from two thousand male "alcohol addicts."[1]

The phase model characterizes the "alcoholic" as generally passing through four phases. These include the prealcoholic symptomatic phase, the prodromal phase, the crucial phase, and the chronic phase. Within these four phases, Jellinek described a list of forty-three behaviors that occur in a somewhat determinant sequence. The prealcoholic symptomatic phase is characterized by a progression from occasional to almost daily relief drinking; that is, drinking to relieve tension. During this phase, individuals develop a tolerance to alcohol and generally drink "fairly heavily," reaching "toward the evening a stage of surcease from emotional stress" (Jellinek, 1962, p. 361). The second phase, the prodromal phase, is marked by "blackouts." These losses of memory occur after a moderate amount of alcohol has been consumed; although persons affected may be able to carry on complex activities, they fail to recall them the following day. Jellinek argued that "average drinkers and non-addictive alcoholics" may also experience "blackouts," but less frequently and after greater alcoholic consumption than "addictive alcoholics." Other behaviors that occur in this phase include surreptitious drinking, gulping of drinks, preoccupation with alcohol, and the development of guilt feelings about drinking behavior. According to Jellinek, "the consumption of alcoholic beverages in the prodromal phase is 'heavy,' but not conspicuous, as it does not lead to marked, overt intoxications. The effect is that the prospective addict reaches toward evening a state which may be designated as emotional anesthesia" (1962, p. 362).

The prodromal phase is followed by the crucial phase. This phase is initiated by loss of control over drinking, that is, "any drinking of alcohol starts a chain reaction which is felt by the drinker as a physical demand for alcohol" (Jellinek, 1962, p. 363). Although drinkers can control whether they will drink or not, they cannot control the quantity once they have initiated drinking. Other characteristics of this phase include aggressive behavior, drinking rationalizations, remorse, periods of abstinence, and morning drinking. During this phase, "intoxication is the rule, but it is limited to the evening hours. For the most part of this phase drinking begins sometime in the afternoon and by the evening intoxication is reached. It should be noted that the 'physical demand' involved in the loss of control results in continual rather than continuous drinking" (Jellinek, 1962, p. 365).

The last phase, the chronic, begins when drinkers can no longer hang on during the daytime and subsequently begin to engage in benders or periods of prolonged intoxication. Other features of this phase include impairment of thinking, indefinable fears, tremors, psychomotor inhibition, and loss of tolerance. During this phase, individuals control these symptoms by drinking.

Jellinek, in summarizing his own research, indicated that the three most commonly occurring behaviors that characterized "alcohol addiction" are blackouts, loss of control, and benders. Blackouts are given additional importance because in the "great majority" of "alcohol addicts," they mark the initial phase, occurring prior to loss of control and benders by many months or years.

Jellinek's model has made important contributions both in terms of its acceptance and influence in the literature and its acceptance by practitioners working with individuals who have drinking problems. "Virtually every book or pamphlet, lay or professional, published in the last 25 years on the manifestations of alcoholism has presented the Jellinekian phases as unchallenged fact" (Goodwin et al., 1969, p. 191). Some writers (Pattison et al., 1977; Lender, 1979; Pokorny and Kanas, 1980; Vaillant, 1983) view Jellinek's phase model and disease definitions of alcoholism as the most profound influence on the alcoholism field to date. Park (1973) regards the phase model as "the most comprehensive and clear-cut ordering of characteristic experiences of alcoholics" (1973, p. 473). Glatt (1970) combined Jellinek's model and his own ideas into a now classically presented, U-shaped progression model of alcoholism that is used worldwide (Pattison et al., 1977).

However, other writers, while still somewhat supportive, have questioned various aspects of the Jellinekian model. Pattison et al. (1977) view Jellinek, A.A., and the National Council of Alcoholism (NCA) as cornerstones of a traditional model of alcoholism that is factually inaccurate but ideologically powerful, a point that I will explore in the next chapter. Albrecht contends that "Jellinek has made such monumental contributions to the study of alcoholism that his shadow has been intimidating to others in the field. . . . There has been a reluctance to challenge or modify some of his basic contributions, even in the face of contrary evidence" (Albrecht, 1973, pp. 18–19). Noticeably more critical is the following attack by Cahalan:

Despite Jellinek's regard for the right of the individual drinker, his conceptions appear to have been subtly influenced by the Protestant ethic. His phases of alcohol addiction, with its orderly—and, inferentially, irreversible—progression of malign symptoms, through the prealcoholic phase, the prodromal phase, the crucial phase, and finally the chronic stage is of a piece with Hogarth's famous illustration of a drunkard's progress on the downward path to perdition. While Jellinek does not say that the phases of alcohol addiction always occur in the same order, his vivid descriptions of the progress of alcoholism are so

84

BECOMING ALCOHOLIC

well attuned to the values of the middle-class Western physician and welfare worker that his cautions are largely overlooked by those who apply his conceptions and by the many writers who repeat his early concepts. (Cahalan, 1970, p. 4)

VERIFICATIONS OF JELLINEK'S MODEL

In addition to these criticisms, there are replicated studies that provide challenging or conflicting evidence as well as specific criticism of Jellinek's formulation. Trice and Wahl's research (1958) examines the methodological aspects of utilizing group averages to depict the patterning of alcoholic behaviors. While the group average might give a general description of the ordering of work, it may, in fact, fit very few of the cases, and it may even distort the typical patterning if, for example, some of the individual scores were highly skewed. Regarding the possible distortion effect, Trice and Wahl comment that "repeated contacts with alcoholics, both in and out of A.A., leave the impression that the 'typical' sequence is not quite typical" (1958, pp. 636–37). Utilizing methodological techniques different from Jellinek's, Trice and Wahl found that there is much "more clustering of symptoms than has been previously assumed" (1958, p. 648). Accordingly, Jellinek's model may not be as sequential as he originally thought.[2] Hoff (1968) and Room (1970) support this view when they criticize tht fit between the real world and Jellinek's model.

Several studies, including Goodwin et al. (1969), dispute the contention that blackouts are the major prodromal symptom of alcoholism. Of the one hundred hospitalized "alcoholics" in their research, one third never experienced a blackout. Additionally, among those who reported blackouts, these generally occurred "well along in the course of alcoholism rather than at an early stage" (Goodwin et al. 1969, p. 191), and they occurred after heavy drinking—"frequently after several days." Other aspects criticized involve the ambiguous nature of the questioning[3] concerning blackouts as well as the occurrence of benders, tremulousness, and severe repercussions from drinking prior to the occurrence of blackouts (1969, p. 195).

Three research efforts appearing in the 1973 *Quarterly Journal of Studies on Alcohol* all failed to support Jellinek's model convincingly.

In fact, two of the three studies posited exploratory descriptions of their own. The first study (Curlee, 1973), hoping to clear up the differences between the Jellinek and Goodwin et al. studies, analyzed the drinking experiences of one hundred patients in the alcoholic treatment unit in the Indianapolis Veterans Administration hospital. The findings more closely resemble Jellinek's in that 83 percent of the respondents reported blackouts. However, in both the Curlee and Goodwin et al. studies, blackouts typically occurred from five (Curlee, 1973) to ten (Goodwin et al., 1969) years later than in Jellinek's research. The second study, Park (1973), stressed the importance of Jellinek's model for both "researchers" and "social control agents" concerned with alcoholism but cautioned that the model "has lacked empirical substantiation and, as a consequence, any judgment as to its usefulness as a practical tool of diagnosis must be held in abeyance" (1973, p. 473). Park utilized data from Finland collected from A.A. clubs, alcoholism clinics, and alcoholism work homes to test Jellinek's ordering of alcoholic experiences. The results depicted an ordering at odds with Jellinek's ordering. Blackouts followed several experiences that they had preceded in Jellinek's analysis. In the third study, Park combined his data with additional data collected by Whitehead. These data were collected in Massachusetts and represented prison inmates, outpatients from alcoholism clinics, patients in the V.A. hospital, and halfway house residents (Park and Whitehead, 1973). This research indicates that, while the Massachusetts data more closely represent Jellinek's formulations than do the Finnish data, there still is considerable disagreement.

More recently, research by Pokorny and Kanas (1980) using V.A. hospitalized alcoholics produced a rank order correlation of .74 between selected symptoms from Jellinek's data and their own. However, this research additionally points out that blackouts occur in nonalcoholic drinkers and that seven out of ten drinkers who experience a blackout will not become alcoholics (Pokorny & Kanas, 1980, p. 66). In fact, for most of the behaviors in Jellinek's phase model, there is overlap between the alcoholic and nonalcoholic samples, and there may be as much variation within alcoholic and nonalcoholic groups as between them. Room's secondary analysis (1978) of various studies in the "Grapevine" tradition finds that there is no overwhelming consistency in the prevalence or ordering of symptoms among samples of persons labeled alcoholic (pp. 56–64).[4]

Social Control Agencies and Alcoholism Models

One major similarity that all of the previously discussed studies have in common is that they drew their data from agencies of social control. Social response theorists since Lemert (1951) have continually argued that social control agency data reflect the operation of the agencies themselves more closely than they reflect rates of deviance. "To accept the label deviant when it is applied to particular acts or people" is to "accept the values of the group making the judgment" (Becker, 1963, pp. 3–4). Jellinek's data (1946, 1952), collected from A.A., are being compared to data from Finnish A.A. clubs, work homes, and alcoholism clinics (Park, 1973), prison clinics, V.A. hospitals, and halfway houses (Park and Whitehead, 1973), medical and detox centers (Goodwin, Crane, and Guze, 1969), more V.A. hospitals (Curlee, 1973; Pokorny and Kanas, 1980), and state hospitals and more A.A. groups (Trice and Wahl, 1958). Obviously, a comparison of data from individuals who are treated and/or detained within diverse settings assumes that alcoholism is a unitary phenomenon and that different social control agencies have the same values; or it assumes that agencies that engage in teaching and socializing their clients have the same effect or no effect upon processes of retrospective interpretation. These must be the assumptions, for none of the studies seems concerned about possible biases that may occur in the processing of cases through the mechanisms of social control. The contamination effect of these social control studies is further complicated because most of the studies utilize respondents who have been involved in a number of social control agencies, sometimes even concurrently. Pokorny and Kanas (1980), for example, selected their alcoholics from the V.A., but most had been involved with A.A. as well.

One study (Trice and Wahl, 1958) mentions the general differences between samples of A.A. affiliates and nonaffiliates in terms of income, occupation, education, etc. However, the authors argue that "these differences seemed to have no consequences for the rank orders" (Trice and Wahl, 1958, p. 638). Yet, on close examination, some differences exist, particularly in terms of the respondents' denial that specific events occurred and their inability to recall such events. Trice and Wahl present the following explanation:

> The non-affiliates tended to deny the onset of symptoms whereas the affiliates manifested a very slight tendency to deny

recall of the dates; . . . the large number of denials of onset
among non-affiliates, if faithful to the facts, describes chronic
excessive drinking with a lower prevalence of complications
than among affiliates. . . . Over three times as many nonaffiliates denied having experienced "frequent blackouts" as did
affiliates. Roughly the same is true for such widely recognized
symptoms as "morning drinking," "loss of control," and "tremors." It seems likely that affiliation with A.A. is, to some degree,
encouraged by having experienced these pronounced symptoms. Certainly the absence of them would lead an excessive
drinker to believe that he was not like other A.A. members.
Without such experiences he would be far less likely to admit
that he was "licked" or that he had a drinking problem. (1958,
p. 646)

The authors' possible explanations for these denial differences are
straightforward; they maintain that the A.A. affiliates have more
complications or that they have fewer rationalizations and better
memories. However, there is another possible explanation for these
differences: members of Alcoholics Anonymous may learn the alcoholic role as A.A. ideology perceives it. A.A. affiliates learn what an
"alcoholic" is from A.A.'s perspective. They learn, if they "qualify,"
how the "diasese" is defined, what behaviors and experiences are
characteristic of alcoholics, and what they must do about their condition. Similar socialization processes occur in other agencies, treatment centers, and hospitals (Bigus, 1974), as well as in A.A. Yet,
while the process remains the same, the content of the message may
change. Members of A.A. may learn that alcoholism is a disease
while persons seeing a clinical psychologist may learn that their
bothersome behavior is a habit or conditioned response that can be
extinguished or diminished. The content and degree of agency socialization is best described by Scott (1969) in his illustration of
blindness as a learned social role.

When those who have been screened into blindness agencies
enter them, they may not be able to see at all or they may have
serious difficulties with their vision. When they have been re-
habilitated, they are all blind men. They have learned the attitudes and behavior patterns that professional blindness workers
believe people should have. In the intensive face-to-face relationships between blindness workers and clients that make up
the rehabilitative process, the blind person is rewarded for
adopting a view of himself that is consistent with his rehabili-

tator's view of him and punished for clinging to other self-conceptions. He is told that he is "insightful" when he comes to describe his problems and his personality as his rehabilitators view them, and he is said to be "blocking" or "resisting" when he does not. Indded, passage through the blindness system is determined in part by his willingness to adopt the expert's view about self. (Scott, 1969, p. 119)

Passage through A.A. is similarly determined. Individuals are more likely to remain in A.A. and to affiliate with the program if their beliefs are supportive of or similar to A.A. ideology (Trice, 1957; Madsen, 1974). A.A. affiliates have diverse drinking experiences. The careers of some members have relatively little drinking and few drinking problems, but many members have serious drinking, physical, and personal problems. In the long run, though, the A.A. socialization experience and the constant give-and-take between A.A. members and between members and sponsors serves to solidify an A.A. persona. Many A.A. members have solidified this persona to such an extent that it is staunchly carried out into their everyday lives. Their views on alcoholism, theories of causation, and models of recovery are the organization's view—the organization's ideology. Yet the question remains: "How, specifically, do A.A. socialization experiences and A.A. ideology affect Jellinek's phase model and its derivatives?"

A.A. SOCIALIZATION AND JELLINEK'S MODEL

Since I have discussed A.A. socialization/affiliation in chapter 2, treatment of this topic will be cursory in this section, except to illuminate those areas that have a direct bearing on my argument—most notably "first stepping" and "qualifying." During these phases of A.A. affiliation, newcomers learn from guides, other members, old-timers, and A.A. literature what "alcoholism" is and if they have it. These messages are further affirmed in testimonials and discussion groups. While communication tends to be two-way, it must be emphasized that active A.A. members are generally viewed by newcomers as the experts. Furthermore, many newcomers, because of pressure from employers, family, significant others, and themselves to affiliate, are susceptible to picking up the message. Do members learn that they are "alcoholics" when they really do not seem to fit contemporary conceptions of "alcoholism?" Obviously yes, in light of the illustrations of tangential and converted alcoholics. Most newcomers fit the organization model in general terms, but a good number do not. Illustrations from two behaviors—blackouts and loss of control—will clarify the argument. These behaviors are particularly important because Jellinek's model maintained that blackouts might be used to differentiate alcoholics from nonalcoholics early in their drinking careers[5] and that loss of control marked movement into the "crucial phase" of alcoholism.

Blackouts are difficult to measure or verify, to say the least. "Asking a person to remember something that by definition involves forgetting, presents formidable problems" (Goodwin et al., 1969, p. 78). In Mideastern City, A.A. members learn the importance of blackouts as a behavior that verifies their alcoholism, and an indeterminable number of members who may not have had blackouts report them. When newcomers to A.A. claim that they cannot remember if they had any blackouts or not, other members use this claim as evidence of the event in question. As one member put it to a newcomer: "The reason you can't remember is because alcohol fogs your brain. If it fogs your brain now after not drinking for a few days it must have fogged your brain before. See, you must have had blackouts then."

The following exchange further illustrates how individuals learn to reinterpret their experiences as symptoms of alcoholism:

FRED: Did you ever blackout?
AL: I don't think so. I passed out a few times.
FRED: Could you remember everything the next day?
AL: No.
FRED: Then it was probably a blackout, too. Blacking out is just like passing out.

This confusion between blackouts and passing out frequently appears in testimonials given at A.A. meetings. Examples include:

The first time I drank, I blacked out and didn't wake up until the next morning.

I first blacked out in high school when I fell off the stage while dancing and didn't come around for a while.

All I was doing was lying in this room, sleeping, drinking, and blacking out.

Blackouts and passing out can be very much the same kind of thing.

Obviously, some of the individuals above may actually have blacked out. The point is that when blacking out is questionable, the group members socialize the newcomer into deciding that he or she did black out. There is no certain way of knowing what percentage of A.A. members have or have not experienced blackouts. However, as Trice and Wahl (1958) and Chandler et al. (1971) illustrate, A.A. members are more likely to report blackouts than are nonaffiliates and Renascence Group members. Although I have emphasized the role of A.A. socialization in recognizing blackouts, it could be that individuals experiencing blackouts are more likely to attend and/or affiliate with A.A. (Goodwin et al., 1969; Trice and Wahl, 1958). This would support the view that filtering mechanisms operate to self-select (bias) the flow of individuals to various alcoholism control agencies. Even if certain symptoms are more likely to be found among "A.A. alcoholics," "V.A. alcoholics," "detox alcoholics," etc., those symptoms are influenced by socialization with significant others, media messages, and agency propaganda. Alcoholism symptoms have been objectified to such a degree that several "yes" answers on alcoholism-typing questionnaires qualify one for the "alcoholic role."

Loss of control is another behavior where there is confusion over meanings. Some members feel that loss of control is a short version of A.A.'s first step, that it is actually the same as being "powerless over alcohol" (Schneider, 1978; Conrad and Schneider, 1980). In a reality reconstruction sense (Schwartz and Jacobs, 1979), A.A. members view loss of control as an explanation or account for "hitting bottom." One hits bottom or one's life becomes unmanageable when one loses control over alcohol. When this occurs, one makes the assessment that one is an alcoholic. Loss of control as described in testimonials and conversations is more a subjective reality or decision than a physiological one. Loss of control is interpreted differently by different people. While alcohologists may be able to define loss of control specifically, the same cannot be said of A.A. members. The following is a testimonial illustrating a member's definition of loss of control:

Alcoholism is a progressive disease. Different people in the program have different experiences, but for all of us, the longer we drank, the worse we got. I'm not exactly sure when alcohol began to take over my life, but I think it is safe to say that I lost control over drinking when I stopped caring about things. All I wanted to do in my spare time was drink.

Another member said: "I wasn't even really aware that I had lost control. Everybody I ran around with was drinking a lot. We got together all the time and when we were together we drank. It was acceptable back then to be drunk. Everybody got drunk." Some A.A. members feel that loss of control is synonymous with not being able to "go on the wagon and stay there." Others feel that loss of control is the same as the "obsessive-compulsive nature" of alcoholism. A middle-aged male in a life-history interview combined several of these themes:

> I knew that I was an alcoholic, that my life was unmanageable, when I lost control over alcohol. Some of us believe that alcoholism involves a mental obsession and a physical compulsion. All I ever thought about before I came into A.A. was drinking. In fact, I was obsessed with thoughts about drinking for a long time after I was in the program. My compulsion for alcohol was there too. I didn't have the shakes or anything, and I'm not sure that it's as simple as an allergy, but there was something physical about needing to drink. I always had this feeling when I was around alcohol or even when I was close to it. When I walked past a bar or ate lunch where booze was served, I felt I had to drink—I just felt it.

A.A. members believe that loss of control is physiological in nature. The behavioral literature strongly refutes this position. Scholarly works (Pattison et al., 1977; Heather and Robertson, 1981) cite more than one hundred research studies that question and in many cases refute traditional models of loss of control. Of particular importance is laboratory research that demonstrated that the level of consumption of alcoholics is shaped by an "instructional set" (what they think they are drinking) rather than the actual beverage administered (Marlatt et al., 1973; Marlatt and Rohsenow, 1981). In another series of experiments (Mello and Mendelson, 1965, 1972; Mendelson and Mello, 1966), environmental contingencies, including the cost and effort required to obtain alcohol, were significant factors in shaping the drinking patterns of chronic alcoholics in in-patient settings.

Overall, it can be said that blackouts and loss of control are two of the three major symptoms that predict alcohol addiction (Jellinek, 1952). These strongly held opinions bias many of the current studies testing and/or formulating phase models in an indeterminable way. These biases are highlighted when data from national probability surveys (Cahalan, 1970; Cahalan and Room, 1974; Clark and Cahalan, 1976) are compared to data and beliefs from phase models. The survey data suggest that alcoholic careers are varied, that they are not as progressive as believed, and that substantial numbers of individuals mature out of drinking problems. Jellinek's model and its contemporary derivatives are, to an unknown degree, reflective of the values of given typing agencies rather than the essential characteristics of alcoholism, if there are any.

Berger and Luckman (1966) view knowledge as constructed through a social enterprise involving externalization, objectivation, and internalization. In my opinion, alcoholism models, particularly those drawn from "samples" of social control agency clients, are constructed belief systems in accordance with Berger and Luckman's model. A.A. members, in developing a practical and applicable theory of alcoholism, come to *believe* through processes of negotiation, interaction, and retrospective interpretation that blackouts, loss of control, and other concepts are useful in making sense of their past lives. More importantly, however, these beliefs are useful in helping individuals define their alcoholism, and they are, in their view, more useful than any previous concept used to solve alcohol problems.

These beliefs, then, were initially A.A. members' externalizations regarding their experiences as alcoholics. They become objectified, that is, they took on a reality of their own, when they were published in A.A. literature and "measured" in the 1946 *Grapevine* questionnaire. Finally, they have reached the level of internalization in contemporary America. Phase models of alcoholism are nearly required socialization material throughout the educational system. Personnel from county alcoholism agencies lecture and administer typing questionnaires to junior and senior high-school students. Communities, high schools, and colleges have yearly alcoholism awareness days or weeks. Newspapers and newsletters carry information regarding the typing of individuals as alcoholics. Jellinek's model is the prototype of reified alcoholism models, not only because his original data were drawn from A.A. members but also because A.A. members were responsible for constructing and administering the initial measuring instrument. An unknown number of A.A. members and other "recovered alcoholics" continue to proselytize phase models with their employment as alcohol counselors—a rapidly expanding occupational category because of federal legislation instituted in the 1970s (Kalb and Propper, 1980; Read, 1981).

To fault A.A. for theoretical and logical limitations of alcoholism models would be to accuse A.A. of being a lousy scientific community. Clinical data, whether from A.A. or elsewhere, are generally incapable of leading to scientific, etiological theories—thus the discrepancy between clinical theories and survey research theories of alcoholism. From a clinical perspective, A.A.'s medical/moral model draws a wide net and serves to promote the organization's attractiveness to a variety of persons. The proliferation of self-help groups using or borrowing A.A. principles is additional testimony of the general applicability of the model.

A.A. does not work for everybody, but then nothing does. A.A. members, on the whole, believe that their approach is certainly the best, if not the only game in town. Such allegiance is consistent with the views of clinicians everywhere. Thinking that one's approach is correct or better than other approaches is an essential feature of the clinician's as well as the client's role. However, it must be a less important feature of the researcher's role if models are to be more than reifications.

7

AN INTERACTIONIST DEFINITION OF
ALCOHOLISM

T HIS STUDY began with a defini-
tion of alcoholics as A.A. members who considered themselves as
such and whose significant others concurred with that assessment.
Using this sensitizing definition, I have described "A.A. alcoholics"
in terms of their accounts, careers, values, and slipping behaviors.
We have also explored some of the links between A.A. and Jellinek's
phase model and the mesh between A.A. alcoholic worlds and sociological worlds. The intent here is to draw together these ideas
through the formulation of a sociological definition of alcoholism.

DEFINING ALCOHOLISM

As Conrad and Schneider (1980) have recently illustrated, and as
many other writers (Matza, 1969; Phillipson, 1971; Szasz, 1970;
Hills, 1977; Rubington and Weinberg, 1978; Thio, 1978; Goode,
1978; Troyer and Markle, 1983; Glassner and Berg, 1984) have also
argued, behavior, whether "deviant" or "not deviant," is usually de-

fined and studied from one of two major theoretical/philosophical approaches—the positivist approach and the interactionist or subjectivist approach. From the positivist approach, alcoholism is real. That is, there is a unitary or diverse list of symptoms, signs, and behaviors that differentiate alcoholics from nonalcoholics and from other drinkers. Through observation and research, positivists maintain that the conditions or causes of alcoholism will be discovered. Failure to discover etiology is always a failure on the researchers' part because their methods are not sophisticated or valid. A positivist explanation for the failure to discover the causes of alcoholism would stress that alcoholism is a complex phenomenon resulting from biological, psychological, and sociological factors. With continued energy and effort, positivists maintain, we will some day discover the causes of this "affliction."

Interactionist/subjectivist approaches emphasize that deviance, in this case "alcoholism," is a relative phenomenon that is constructed in given situations and in given historical time frames by participants. "Alcoholism" is a historical and political accomplishment (Schneider, 1978; Conrad and Schneider, 1980). For interactionists, "alcoholism" is a category, label, or imputation that is made about or attached to persons by others. Mulford and Miller (1960) state:

> It goes without saying that there are "alcoholics." Certain people are so labeled every day. But it does not necessarily follow that there is an alcoholism entity. The present study has assumed that "alcoholism" is a term referring to a constellation or configuration of behaviors which, when manifested by an individual, render him a likely candidate for the label "alcoholic." (Mulford and Miller, 1960, p. 188)

From an interactionist perspective, "alcoholism" is what it is taken to be by given people in given situations. The meaning of phenomena from this perspective is a consequence of the definitions and meanings that are attached to them by actors. "Alcoholism exists in our language and in our minds, but not in the objective world around us" (Rohan, 1978, p. 211). According to Armor et al., "'alcoholism' and 'becoming an alcoholic' are very much what people take them to be when they employ such notions in the course of their everyday lives" (1978, p. vii). One of the major themes behind the interactionist perspective is that deviance is best viewed as collective action. Accordingly, designations of deviance involve interaction and negotiation between actors and others. From an interactionist perspective, deviant designations are best viewed as outcomes or culminations of many collective actions between participants. That is to say that deviance is a process in which behaviors, perceptions of behaviors, and actors are defined by themselves and/or others as deviant.

Positivistic Definitions

Positivist definitions, because they make assertions about phenomena that are measurable or inferable, are subject to truth claims (Bierstedt, 1959). Thus, positivist definitions differ from nominalist definitions that conventionally allow a word to stand for an idea or an object. Frequently, nominal definitions of phenomena become so familiar that, through processes of objectification (Berger and Luckman, 1966) and reification, they become treated as real. I argued in the last chapter that the most dominant of contemporary positivist definitions of alcoholism is not a positivist definition at all, but a reification.

Pattison et al. (1977) summarize what they perceive as the essential characteristics of the traditional model of alcoholism. In their opinion, the traditional model views alcoholism as a permanent, irreversible, progressive disease characterized by craving and loss of control (Pattison et al., 1977, pp. 2–26). After systematically examining research related to the major assumptions of this traditional view, Pattison and his colleagues concluded that the model does not fit the experiences of people in the real world. Specifically, all characteristics of the traditional model are challenged and questioned if existing alcohol and alcoholism research is highlighted. Clearly, there is a major disjunction between the normative and factual levels of alcoholism and alcoholism information. As a result, the gulf between what people in this society believe and what we know about alcoholism is extreme. Furthermore, this gulf is nearly as severe when we compare what we know with what our alcoholism models assume or what our alcoholism practitioners believe. As a number of writers have argued (Szasz, 1970; Schneider, 1978; Room, 1978; Conrad and Schneider, 1980; Beauchamp, 1980; Heather and Robertson, 1981), the medical or positivistic model of alcoholism is a

historical and political accomplishment. Jellinek's contemporary re-
vival (1960) of the disease definition was intended as a speculative,
working hypothesis and not as a scientific model. Unfortunately, in
their haste to understand and ameliorate alcohol problems, Jellinek
and others lost sight of their initial cautions.

I believe that A.A. alcoholics and their theoretical stereotypes,
symbolized by the Jellinekian phase model of alcoholism, are merely
the most highly emphasized and most powerful definitions of alcoholism in the United States today.[1] They are powerful in the sense
that E. M. Jellinek has written more about alcoholism than has any
other individual, that A.A. has been successful in leading some
drinkers to sobriety, and that the alcoholism movement has been
receptive to A.A. ideology. The A.A. definition and its emphasis on
disease and allergy are popular because they enable persons involved
with problem drinkers to understand or accept their drinking. When
members of a society engage in strange behavior, other members of
that society frequently proclaim that the norm violators are sick
(Szasz, 1970). The application of such a label makes strange behavior more palatable, and the sickness label also informs one of the
possibilities for treatment (Scheff, 1966; Szasz, 1970; and Conrad,
1975). When significant others cannot understand individuals who
engage in strange drinking behavior, they frequently settle for the
A.A. definition of alcoholic.[2] In essence, labelers and laypersons in
this society are so confused and frustrated about alcoholism that they
are perfectly willing to call it a disease and hope that it will go away.
On a logical level, drinking alcohol, even excessive amounts of alcohol, is no more a disease than smoking cigarettes. If a person
smokes enough or if a person drinks enough, he or she might develop
a disease like emphysema, lung cancer, cirrhosis, or organic brain
damage, but to say that excessive smoking or drinking is a disease is
to confuse a disease with its cause (Szasz, 1966).

If alcoholism is not a disease, then why do so many laypersons
and alcoholism professionals call it that? Jellinek found the following
answer:

> Physicians know what belongs in their realm. . . . It comes to
> this, that a *disease is what the medical profession recognizes as
> such.* The fact that they are not able to explain the nature of a
> condition does not constitute proof that it is not an illness.
> There were many instances in the history of medicine of disease

whose nature was unknown, but they are, nevertheless, un-
questionably medical problems. (Jellinek, 1960, p. 23)

What Jellinek failed to note is that, like most of us, physicians
make errors. For example, Benjamin Rush, the father of American
psychiatry, viewed "negritude" as a special type of leprosy. Rush also
viewed lying, murdering, and minority group dissent as mental ill-
nesses (Szasz, 1970, pp. 137–59). It is also interesting that Rush is
responsible for the "first clearly developed modern conception of
alcohol addiction" (Levine, 1978, p. 151). At various later dates,
American physicians have viewed drug addiction, hyperactivity, suicide, obesity, crime, violence, political dissent, and child abuse as
worthy of disease labels and hence treatment by physicians. Szasz
(1970) and more recently Conrad (1975, 1976) and Conrad and
Schneider (1980) view this broadening social control function of
medicine as the "medicalization of deviance." Medical and other
constructions of alcohol problems are an ever-increasing part of the
contemporary alcohol literature (Room, 1978; Levine, 1978; Beauchamp, 1980; Wiener, 1981; Gusfield, 1981). Each of these writers
emphasizes how historical, political, and ideological factors give rise
to what Room calls "governing images" of alcohol and alcohol problems. Room (1978) articulates three contemporary governing images—the classic disease model, an "ambivalence" model, and an
epidemic model—that are important in understanding alcoholism
policy in the United States during the past forty to fifty years.
    In arguing that progressive disease models of alcoholism are nom-
inal definitions turned real and that disease models are reifications,
I am not saying that disease models are worthless. I am not saying
that clinically or in A.A. no one has been "helped." As Roizen (1978)
points out, alcoholism theories can be evaluated on at least two major dimensions—their "correctness" and their utility. Progressive disease models have *some* utility but *little* correctness.
    Other positivistic definitions of alcoholism are more correct than
progressive disease models. For example, Wallgren and Herbert view
alcoholism and more specifically the "phenomenon" of loss of control as a habit (1970, pp. 740–53). These writers and others (Conger,
1956, 1958; Akers, 1985), using basic principles from learning
theory, emphasize that anxiety avoidance and negative reinforcement allow some drinkers to develop a habit of excessive drinking.

This behavior occurs in those settings where the individual can successfully use alcohol to reduce anxiety or stress. Heather and Robertson's *Controlled Drinking* (1981) summarizes substantial research that seriously challenges conceptions of loss of control and craving. These writers argue that a learning theory/behaviorist approach is in the process of replacing the medical/disease model as the dominant paradigm in alcohol thought and research. Their optimism is easily shared in rational intellectual debate, but such debate is infrequently found in the political arenas of social problem construction (Wiener, 1981). The best positivistic sociological work is represented by Cahalan and his colleagues of the Berkeley Social Research Group. Cahalan (1970) and Cahalan and Room (1974), rather than trying to make an absolute distinction between alcoholics and nonalcoholics, study drinking behavior and "problems associated with drinking behavior." Such an approach highlights that drinking, as well as problems with drinking, is best viewed on continua (Cahalan et al., 1969).

An Interactionist Definition

Rather than addressing the essential characteristics of alcoholism or alcoholics, interactionist definitions emphasize the processes and structures involved in specific social contexts that lead to the social designation of actors as "alcoholics." *Alcoholism is a characterization attached to drinkers by others when these others question the drinkers' behavior and when the drinkers lack the power or desire to negotiate another explanation.* Since actors have the ability to reflect upon themselves and take the role of others toward themselves, it is logically and empirically possible for persons to label themselves and question their own drinking. This definition emphasizes the two essential elements of all interactionist definitions—behavior and societal response (Becker, 1963, 1973).

Before we examine this definition in detail, the reader must be aware that it is not the same to say that alcoholism is a characterization that involves behavior and response as it is to say that alcoholism is sin, moral weakness, crime, or illness. The latter definitions are definitions of phenomena as social problems while the former is a sociological definition. The latter definitions imply the designation of alcoholism as a social problem, along with a general perspective on what should be done about it—that it be treated, punished, etc. Additionally, these definitions imply that alcoholism is different from grace, moral strength, normal behavior, and health. The sociological definition, on the other hand, immplies that alcoholism is behavior and that, accordingly, it will share many of the characteristics that one expects to observe in any type of behavior. For example, individual predispositions and perceptions, as well as social norms and situational constraints, will shape the character of the behavior. In turn, these factors interact in some not clearly known way with the pharmacological properties of the drug, ethyl alcohol.

The definition of alcoholism as an imputed characterization highlights the relativity of deviance and alcoholism. Drinking norms are relative to given groups, subcultures, and situations. If "others' questioning" is included as a focal point, reference points that are pertinent in defining drinking behavior as alcoholism within various social systems are maintained.

Another focal point of the definition is that drinkers frequently accept the characterization for lack of power. According to Rubington (1973), "alcoholism cannot raise a man's status" (1973, p. 49). The label alcoholic in Becker's terminology (1963) qualifies one as an "outsider." For Goffman (1962), alcoholism is conceptualized as a type of stigma or a "deeply discrediting attribute." Accordingly, the label alcoholic is not likely to be an object of striving.[3] Rather, it is something to be avoided. When A.A. members received queries about their drinking from family and friends as well as from formal agents of social control, their typical response in Mideastern City was denial. Mideastern City A.A. members try to negotiate other explanations for their drinking behavior. Typical answers illustrative of this denial include:

How can I be an alcoholic? I have a family, a house, a job. . . . I know I drink quite a bit, but I'm not an alcoholic.

Doctor, I may be crazy or insane, but I'm not an alcoholic.

Sure I drink a lot, but I have good reason to. If I didn't have all these problems, I wouldn't be drinking.

Maybe sometimes I drink too much and maybe I can't hold my liquor that well, but that doesn't make me an alcoholic.

All of these statements illustrate a common strategy: when individuals are questioned about their drinking, they try to neutralize their deviance by using justifications and denials (Lyman and Scott, 1970) that do not implicate them as secondary deviants (alcoholics). When Mideastern City A.A. members accept the characterization "alcoholic," they do so typically because they have no other feasible course of action, because they lack power to control their lives and activities, or because they are forced by others with more power to accept the label alcoholic.

When individuals have problems associated with their drinking—the loss of jobs or spouses, beating their children, absenteeism, arguments with spouses, depression, etc.—they are expected to give accounts of their behavior. When the accounts deny, justify, or neutralize their behavior, their drinking is primary. As long as behavior is explained in terms of various aspects of socially approved roles, the deviance remains primary or situational (Lemert, 1951). The deviance becomes secondary, that is, problems with alcohol became alcoholism, when the individual "begins to employ his deviant behavior or a role based upon it as a means of defense, attack, or adjustment to the overt and covert problems created by consequent societal reaction to him" (Lemert, 1951, p. 75). The distinction between primary and secondary alcoholics, although important to labeling theorists in sociology, may be even more important to clinicians and to persons experiencing problems with and from drinking since engulfment into an "alcoholic role" is likely to solidify the drinker's problems with alcohol and to increase further the gulf between drinkers and significant others (Kinsey, 1966; Roman and Trice, 1968; Bacon, 1973).

Contingencies not only shape the likelihood of acceptance of an alcoholic characterization, they also affect the probability that the characterization will be offered in the first place. Contingencies affecting others' responses include the level, style, and visibility of consumption; the location and consequences of drinking; the geographic locale; the occupational status; and numerous other factors. Goffman (1961) argued that, in a specific sense, contingencies are responsible for institutionalizing persons as mentally ill. The same can be said about "alcoholism" processing. Estimates of "alcoholics" indicate that for every "treated" or "discovered alcoholic" there are five or six "hidden alcoholics." These individuals remain outside of

the population of discovered alcoholics because they possess contingencies that are effective in reducing role engulfment. They are able
to manage their drinking behavior successfully and to negotiate other
explanations should their drinking be questioned. Drinkers from up-
per social strata are likely to have more to negotiate with; hence, they
are less likely to be processed than are drinkers from lower strata. All
other things being equal, contingencies are dominant predictors of
"becoming alcoholic" (Keil et al., 1983).

Once a drinker is characterized as an alcoholic, a number of logical and empirical consequences can occur. The individual may try
to negotiate a different characterization, as in the case of the person
who explains his or her drinking as due to increased personal problems, pressure, drinking situations, or the like. In short, the drinking
is viewed as a result of an unusual situation and not unusual or
deviant in and of itself. An "accused alcoholic" might deny his or
her characterization as an alcoholic. One speaker at an open meeting
said:

> I really didn't believe that I was an alcoholic. Some of my
> friends and my wife said they were worried about my drinking,
> and they thought that I had a problem; but I didn't believe it. I
> was doing well at work. I didn't drink in the morning. Sure I
> drank a lot, but I wasn't an alcoholic. I liked to drink, and I
> thought that drinking helped me relax and unwind; there was
> always a lot of pressure in my business [sales].

Another possible response to an alcoholic characterization is acceptance of the designation. In this case, drinkers use the characterization to increase engulfment into an alcoholic role and to increase
their drinking; or drinkers may use the characterization as a reason
to seek help or attempt to stop drinking. A typical illustration of how
persons use acceptance of an alcoholic designation to continue their
drinking is found in the comment of a south-side group member
who said that "that was all I needed—to be told that I was an alcoholic. If that is what I was, I thought I might as well get a bottle and
get on with it and forget about everything else." Other Mideastern
City A.A. members further illustrate the same theme with similar
statements: "If I was an alcoholic, it was only natural that I spend my
time drinking"; "When friends called me an alcoholic I said, 'Sure,
now fill it up.'"

While it is clear that the response of others reinforced some members' drinking, it also led others to stop. The general likelihood of continuing versus stopping as a response to labeling is shaped by many of the contingencies mentioned earlier. From a behavioral orientation, it might be said that drinkers continue on the path that is most rewarding or least painful. That is, if it is less costly and less painful to continue drinking, the person will choose this option. From the point of view of A.A., individuals who continue drinking after labeling have not hit bottom yet.

All of the actors' possible responses as well as the responses of others to drinking characterizations are built into our belief system regarding "alcoholic behavior" and "alcoholic responses." In this regard, much of what "alcoholics" and significant others do, say, and think in regard to drinking characterizations is influenced by scripts, expectations, and beliefs. In fact, most of the behaviors we have been describing are role behaviors that are a consequence of a person's given status within a structure. For example, the drama of alcoholism characterizations includes persons who drink and persons who define persons who drink as "problem drinkers" or "alcoholics." These definers may be formal (psychiatrists, alcoholism counselors, and the like) or informal (spouses, family members, friends). To the extent that an alcoholic designation is disvalued, people try to avoid the designation. Accordingly, as a function of avoiding the designation, drinkers may hide their drinking. This behavior is a consequence of the position that the actors occupy. It is not a consequence of the personality structures of "alcoholics." Frequently, significant others may also try to cover or hide the problem that their friends or family members are experiencing with alcohol. Should they help out, the drinker is more likely to become dependent—another presumably "alcoholic behavior."

Even behaviors that are assumed to be a direct consequence of the human organism's response to alcohol—for example, drunken behavior and drinking to reduce the pain of withdrawal—are in part role behaviors. Individuals learn different scripts or roles about acting drunk, and they learn about responding to the pain of withdrawal. In fact, one of the ways in which people act drunk when they are not supposed to be drunk is, in fact, to act sober. In other words, drinkers tend to mask their drinking and drunkenness. To the extent that persons' responses are a consequence of cultural or subcultural recipes for action, they are role behaviors. Such scripts, coupled with definitions and meanings held by actors that also influence their action, are probably stronger determinants of action toward alcohol and of action under the influence of alcohol than are the properties of ethyl alcohol. Research by Sugarman (1974) among "heroin addicts" supports this argument. Sugarman argues that "cold turkey withdrawal" from heroin in therapeutic drug communities is similar to a mild flu and very much unlike withdrawal in hospital or private settings. The general point is that drug-related behavior is probably more a consequence of situations, definitions, and meanings than of the properties of given drugs (Becker, 1953, 1967; Goode, 1984).

IMPLICATIONS

Of what implication is the statement that alcoholism is a characterization and that much alcohol-related behavior is role behavior? First of all, it highlights what Goode (1984) refers to as the chemicalistic fallacy, that is, that a given drug causes a given type of behavior. There is nothing within the drug alcohol that directly causes humans to act in certain ways. While certain motor responses and organic changes are clearly predictable, behavior is not (MacAndrew and Edgerton, 1969). Other researchers have documented that societal values determine the existence or nonexistence of alcoholism and hangovers in various societies (Lemert, 1954; Heath, 1962) and that norms regarding drinking behavior are more influential in determining and predicting drunken behavior than are the physiological properties of alcohol (MacAndrew and Edgerton, 1969). Additionally, Spradley (1970) illustrated that the societal response to public drunkenness is a cause rather than a cure of public drunkenness. Each of these social scientists argued that sociological variables such as values, norms, and societal responses are more important in shaping alcohol usage and alcoholic careers than is the drug alcohol itself.[4] While these studies deal with public drunkenness offenders (Spradley, 1970), Northwest Coast Indians (Lemert, 1954), and various other cultures (MacAndrew and Edgerton, 1969), my research utilized primarily middle-class Americans participating in a self-help program for alcoholics. There is no reason to believe that drinking behavior in any social context is not highly shaped by social and psychological factors.

In saying that much alcohol related behavior is role behavior, we are also asserting that the various attitudes and patterns of behavior that individuals labeled as alcoholics manifest are acquired through the ordinary processes of socialization and learning and are not inherent in their condition, that is, their alcoholism. Interaction with significant others, public stereotypes of alcoholics, media presentations of labeling material, the learning of drinking styles and practices, and social control agency definitions and assumptions regarding alcoholism feed into a process in which behaviors and definitions of behaviors are shaped into alcoholism characterizations. Recently, over two million copies of "Here's Looking at You: The American Drinker" were distributed through large urban newspapers (National Institute on Alcohol Abuse and Alcoholism, November 23, 1976). This tabloid presented "facts" on alcohol, an interview with a recovered alcoholic, an alcoholic crossword puzzle, and information on where to get help for alcoholism. Information and misinformation are disseminated not only through newspapers but through the other media as well. If one couples the media bombardment of information and misinformation regarding alcoholism with the messages of regional and local alcohol treatment centers, it becomes clear that frequent and powerful messages are being transmitted that clarify and simplify drinking behavior into a stock category called alcoholism.

Freidson's (1965) discussion of disability as deviance adds to this argument that alcoholism is a learned social role and that the role is defined by treatment centers.

> Both professionalism and bureaucratization objectify and reify diagnostic categories. In this sense, while such agencies may not actually create deviant roles, they do by the nature of their activities refine and clarify their boundaries and, by assuming responsibility for their control, add elements to the roles that may not have existed previously, and so encourage pulling new people into them. (Freidson, 1965, p. 83)

Agency practitioners pull more and more people into their nets for a variety of reasons. First, in their desire to alleviate social problems, they may become overzealous. Second, as Scheff (1966, 1984) argues, medical practitioners and medical social control agencies are more likely to diagnose disease when, in fact, the person is healthy as opposed to diagnosing health when the person suffers from disease.[5] Third, since more people drink in American society today than in past years (Cahalan and Room, 1974), there may be a commensurate increase in problem drinking. Finally, by processing large numbers of individuals, agencies prove their worth and can legitimize their request for further financial support to continue and/or expand their operations. Whatever the reasons, when large numbers of problem drinkers are processed through various treatment programs, many of them begin to manifest the same patterns or the same retrospective interpretations that Scott (1969) so accurately described in *The Making of Blind Men*. According to Scott, "people who initially think of themselves as sighted people who have trouble seeing come to think of themselves as blind people who have residual vision. Blindness becomes the primary factor around which they organize their lives and in terms of which they relate to other people" (1969, pp. 120–21).

In Mideastern City A.A., individuals who manifest a wide variety of drinking behaviors ranging from stereotypical skid-row drinking to very little drinking at all come to think of themselves as alcoholics. It is not that deviant drinking, or in Cahalan's terms (1970) "Problem drinking," does not exist. Rather, it is that specific social control agencies attach to complex and varied drinking careers an oversimplistic model of alcoholism that does not fit. While such beliefs (myths) may assist some persons in "recovering" from alcoholism, they have numerous deleterious consequences when misapplied.

8

ALCOHOLIC WORLDS AND
SOCIOLOGICAL WORLDS

I$_N$ CHAPTER 6, I argued that Jelli-
nek's phase model of alcoholism and the A.A. model of alcoholism
are one and the same and that they are constructions or reifications
of A.A. values. Chapter 7 criticized the medical or disease model of
alcoholism and developed a relativistic interactionist definition of
alcoholism. In this chapter, I will again rely on members' accounts
to draw out some final themes from Mideastern City A.A. Additionally, I will integrate some of the broader sociological literature on
problem drinking and alcoholism[1] with the views of A.A. members.

Alcoholism as a term attached to some persons by others or by
themselves and as a theoretical construct in the sociological literature
is the product of reality construction. Depending upon a group's
value system,[2] definitions regarding alcohol use, both normal and
deviant, are developed and utilized to make sense out of the world.
Some groups and societies have constructed alcoholism definitions
and meanings for some types of drinking behavior while others have
not (Bunzel, 1940; MacAndrew and Edgerton, 1969; Heath, 1981).

The diversity of cultural differences in drinking practices (Marshall, 1979) is matched by the diversity of cultural views in defining deviant drinking practices. Theoretical constructions of alcohol use, alcohol abuse, and alcoholism, like real world constructions, are also shaped by values and assumptions regarding one's academic discipline, funding sources, theoretical presuppositions, political ideology and the like. For sixteen months, I came to know about alcoholism by sharing some of Mideastern City A.A.'s world with its members. I have also "experienced" alcoholism from reading the theoretical and research literature of sociologists. In the following section, I will explore these worlds simultaneously, using a few A.A. slogans as organizational tools.

"ASKING WHY"

Mideastern City A.A. members frequently comment that "to ask why is the wrong question." Figuring out why one is an alcoholic or why A.A. works is "analyzing not utilizing." One old-timer summarized what most A.A. members know: "Some alcoholics have high bottoms and some have low bottoms, and some never hit bottom—they just die." Mideastern City A.A. members know firsthand that alcoholics come in all shapes and sizes. Some A.A. members are "high-class drunks" and some "take skid row home with them." Pure alcoholics and convinced alcoholics, as described in chapter 4, have careers characterized by heavy drinking and extraordinary problems associated with their drinking. Converted and tangential alcoholics have careers with less heavy alcohol use. A few of these members probably drank very little. Some Mideastern City A.A. members approach the program so totally defeated, stigmatized, and alone, so hurt, that there is no intellectualizing about their alcoholism. Others approach the program with families, friends, and careers intact and spend months trying A.A. out.

Drawing from my experience with A.A. members and my view of the general literature in the sociology of deviance, I believe that there are as many ways of "becoming alcoholic" as there are of becoming anything. Deviant (alcoholic) careers are different from normal careers in the sense that they are negatively valued by most members of society and that they are *always* the focus of microscopic explanation. Many persons have dedicated their lives to exploring the biologies, psychologies, and sociologies of alcoholics and criminals in search of etiological factors. Few people explore the anatomies, thought patterns, and life experiences of physicians, pipe fitters, and sociologists. This is not to equate going to work with going to drink! However, from a career perspective, going to work is essential to a work career, and drinking is essential to an alcoholic career. There are many why's that "explain" work: I like to work; I like my job; I'll lose my house; I'll lose my job; work makes me feel good; I need to work. There are many why's that explain drinking: I like to drink; drinking makes me feel good; I need to drink; I'll hurt if I don't drink; drinking makes me feel powerful; I'm an alcoholic.

From a pharmacological viewpoint, alcohol is a psychoactive drug in that it can affect the drinker's emotion, thought, perception, and feeling. However, the ways in which the pharmacological properties of alcohol interact with and are modified by drinkers' psychologies, drinking settings, and culture remain vague and speculative. From observing "recovered alcoholics" in A.A. and from reading the current debate in alcohology, I do not know what an alcoholic really is. My frame of reference here is positivism.[3] Keller's comments on the oddities of alcoholics strike me in general as true for the oddities of all deviants: "Alcoholics are different in so many ways that it makes no difference" (1972, p. 1147). Keller's comparison is between alcoholics and other groups, and it points out that microscopic investigation repeatedly shows that alcoholics will have more or less of any trait when compared to control populations. My point is that the differences between individuals who came to view themselves as alcoholics are equally great. As A.A. members say, "To ask why is the wrong question."

Just as there is no clearly definable way that leads into an alcoholic career, there is no single way out of it. However, entry into an alcoholic career is much easier than exit. Personally, if I viewed myself as an alcoholic, I would go the A.A. and abstinence route. My experience tells me that it works for quite a few of those who try it and that most A.A. members who strongly commit themselves to the life style are happy. Intellectually and factually, other approaches are possible. The war regarding controlled drinking has escalated since Davies' report (1962) of normal drinking in a small number of "recovered alcohol addicts." The most current battle[4] concerns a follow-up study by Pendery et al. (1982) of research by the Sobells (Sobell,

1978; Sobell and Sobell, 1978; Caddy et al., 1978). These research teams disagree regarding teaching "moderate drinking" skills to alcoholics.[5] Unfortunately, the media clamor over this dispute and its corresponding court case may detract from recent overviews of the controlled drinking research (Miller, 1980; 1983; Heather and Robertson, 1981). These latter works systematically point out that a range of approaches and treatment modalities, from controlled drinking to abstinence, is validated in the contemporary literature on alcoholism treatment.

"ALCOHOLIC THINKING"

"Alcoholism is not only a drinking disease, it's a thinking disease." Mideastern City A.A. members routinely reflect this and related views in testimonials and conversations. "Alcoholic thinking," sometimes called "stinking thinking," is the term that members use to describe how they used to think about alcohol and drinking. Sometimes these terms are also used to describe current negative or bad thinking that could lead to the "first drink." During a testimonial at an open meeting, the speaker, Steve, commented:

> Drinking was wiping out my stomach. My doctor told me that if I kept drinking, my ulcer would get worse. Now, anybody with any sense would have quit drinking, but I was an alcoholic—I didn't have any sense. I decided that I needed a drink, so I went out to a bar and ordered bourbon and milk. I figured that then I would be okay. Now, that's what I call alcoholic thinking. Only an alcoholic would drink bourbon and milk and think it was normal.

Another testimonial speaker, Roger, said:

> By this time I was divorced, and I kept running into trouble because I wasn't making my child support payments. My wife would call the sheriff, and I would be picked up and charged, and the judge kept putting me in jail because I wasn't paying. To show you how warped my thinking was then: One night, when I was drinking, I kept thinking that the payments were really getting me down. Like a flash it came to me, if my wife wouldn't call the sheriff then I wouldn't get in trouble. I went to my nightstand, loaded my pistol and got in the car and headed for Openville. Right, I was going to drive four hundred

miles and shoot my wife, so I wouldn't have to pay child support. With thinking like that you don't need any enemies.

Any reason or justification to continue drinking, positive beliefs about drinking, denial, and rationalizations, all can be seen as "alcoholic thinking." How and what actors think about alcohol and drinking has been a dominant theme in the alcohol literature since the 1940s. Research studies (Riley et al., 1948; Mulford and Miller, 1959, 1960; Cahalan, 1970) demonstrate that "personal effects" attitudes toward drinking, alcohol preoccupation, and other perceptual variables relate to problem drinking and high-quantity and high-frequency drinking. Jellinek's phase model views the drinker's definitions and redefinitions of alcohol use and drinking situations as related to "alcoholic progression" (Jellinek, 1952). Attitudes toward drinking and other factors have been used to explain the relative absence of Jews from problem-drinking data. Extending Snyder's work (1958), Glassner and Berg (1980) describe how, through informal controls, Jews define alcohol problems as non-Jewish, learn drinking practices and beliefs early in childhood, reinforce these practices in adult peer groups, and practice evasive strategies to avoid heavier drinking in situations where social pressures encourage it (Glassner and Berg, 1980, pp. 653–63). Such definitions and collective strategies insulate most Jews from drinking problems.

"Giving It Away"

For A.A. members, sobriety is something that one must work at. A.A. members earn or gain sobriety through sharing their "experience, strength, and hope" with others. "Giving it away" has a variety of interpretations in Mideastern City A.A., but the bottom line is sharing oneself with another person. This can be accomplished through twelfth-step work, twelfth-step calls, telling one's story, inventory taking, and a variety of other possibilities. "Giving it away," for many A.A. members, marks a return to social life. Many A.A. careers are characterized by an ever-increasing "obsession and compulsion" with alcohol and drinking. Drinking becomes the organizing feature of their lives. Maxwell (1984) uses the term "the drinking relationship" to characterize this all-encompassing life style for some A.A. members. Mideastern City A.A. members, in the context of discussion meetings said:

Alcohol was my life. I couldn't handle not drinking, so I just dropped out and drank.

I didn't care if the bills were paid or not or if the rent was met. All I cared about was drinking.

All I wanted to do was drink—nothing else.

My life revolved around drinking. It seemed that nothing else mattered.

I didn't care about anybody or anything. I heard someone say once that they "loved to drink and drank to live." That's how I felt. At its worst, I don't think I had any emotion about anybody, not even myself.

The loneliness and isolation of these explanations are the exact opposite of the sharing, love, and involvement of the typical A.A. setting. A.A. members frequently describe in testimonials the warmth, intimacy, caring and sharing that typify the "fellowship of A.A." Perhaps the A.A. society's reestablishment of social relationships (Bales, 1945; Robinson, 1976; Kurtz, 1979, Curlee-Salisbury, 1982; Vaillant, 1983; Maxwell, 1984) indicates weak social relations among many heavy drinkers. The views of contemporary sociologists (Snyder, 1964; Trice and Roman, 1972; Bacon, 1973; Mizruchi and Perrucci, 1973; Rubington, 1973; Cahalan, 1978) indicate that weakened interpersonal support systems, permissive and ambivalent sanctioning responses, normalization of deviant drinkers by others, and withdrawal are factors contributing toward the development of drinking problems. From Bacon's point of view (1973), the responses of others can make or break the continuation of deviant drinking. Typical responses of others to Mideastern City A.A. members' previous drinking include the following:

Once I got a ten dollar fine for driving while intoxicated. A few days after it happened, I talked to a judge and he told me that if I had appeared before him, he would have given me my ten dollars back.

My family tolerated my drinking.

My mother probably knew I was drinking, but since I wasn't taking the car, she wasn't worried. So she never really said anything about my drinking.

I had to be interviewed by the new section chief, and the night before I went out and got clobbered. I was sicker than ever, and that day I went out for lunch and started once again. Instead of letting me be interviewed, my friends shuffled me around the office, trying to hide me.

My mother knew I was drinking, but I think all she really worried about was my passing high school

Even when I was a kid, it was the same. You weren't supposed to do this [drink], but it made you feel good, and we all did it. All through my life, it was like that: you weren't supposed to get drunk but people did. . . . When you drank too much or got sick or whatever, your friends and family helped you cover it. A lot of my buddies at work drank a lot too. . . . For a long time, I thought I could handle it. I was having a good time, but later I paid the price. I guess I just didn't know when to quit.

By the time others respond to drinking problems, it is usually too late, and the way in which they respond—exclusion—is not very effective (Trice, 1966; Bacon, 1973; Bigus, 1974; Trice and Roman, 1972). The following conversational account from a west-end member describes this situation:

TED: When my friends started telling me that I was drinking too much, I thought that they were all wet. Sure I drank a lot, but so did a lot of other guys. Then when some of them started avoiding me, I thought it was because they thought they were too good for me. I had other problems too, but at the time I didn't think any of them were because of my drinking. In fact, the way I saw it, I could handle my drinking. I didn't regard it as a problem

DAVE: So when did it become a problem?

TED: Now, I know it was a problem even then, but at the time, I just thought I liked to drink a lot—like a lot of other guys I knew. I wasn't even sure that it was a problem when I first had trouble with my job.

DAVE: What do you mean?

TED: Well, I was progressing well on my work, but I did have a couple of auto accidents. It was at this time that I began to think that I was drinking more than was good for me. I further decided, or had a feeling, that my drinking was becoming a problem because I was put on another shift at work, and I felt that maybe my work capabilities were less. My

> drinking . . . well most of the time I didn't get drunk. I just
> kind of had a steady glow, just enough to make me feel a little
> better. Maybe once or twice a week, I would get drunk.

Another member, during a life history, told me:

> It's too late now, but something that always bothers me is that
> nobody told me. Nobody told me how destructive alcohol
> could be. If I had known that all these things that happened to
> me were going to happen, maybe it would have been different.
> Nobody ever said, "Be careful," or anything. People know how
> bad alcohol can be, but nobody talks about it.

These statements and excerpts illustrate responses to drinking and
drunkenness in situations where drinking and drunkenness were proscribed but yet responded to with tolerance or permissiveness. Such
conditions force individuals to carve out for themselves a system of
values, meanings, and goals regulating their use of alcohol. In a
society where ideas regarding alcohol use are ambivalent (Myerson,
1940),[6] contradictory, and inconsistent, this is no easy task. On a
normative level, drinking is against the law for persons under the
ages of eighteen to twenty-one, contingent upon state statutes and
type of beverages consumed; but substantial numbers of young
people drink illegally (Cahalan and Room, 1974; Blane and Hewitt,
1977; Johnston et al., 1981). On the normative level, drunkenness
is legally proscribed while one operates a motor vehicle or in public
settings. It is also more broadly proscribed in a variety of subcultural
normative systems, but substantial numbers of Americans, both ado-
lescents and adults, drink frequently to intoxication (Cahalan, 1970;
Cahalan and Room, 1974; Johnston et al., 1981); and many subcultural contexts emphasize the ability to "hold one's liquor like a man"
as a valued model. When sanctions as well as norms are inconsistent
and ambiguous, problems regarding the phenomenon in question
are assured for the society (Rubington, 1973).

There are few shortcuts to sobriety. A.A. members routinely testify
that sobriety is a lifelong process. There are few shortcuts or easy
solutions to drinking problems in American society. Current public
health approaches emphasize decreasing alcohol consumption per
capita[7] through measures including advertising restrictions, increased taxation, and a higher legal minimum drinking age (Beauchamp, 1980, pp. 152–82; Wagenaar, 1983). Such policies may

reduce problem drinkers and alcohol-related problems, but not drastically. For example, Wagenaar (1983) estimates that raising the minimum drinking age to twenty-one will reduce alcohol-related traffic
fatalities involving young persons by about twenty percent. Perhaps
once we understand that "law making is not behavior making"
(Keller, 1982) and that television commercials, product labeling, and
drug education programs in our schools still leave us with an alcohol
problem, we will begin to think about drinking and drinking problems differently (Gusfield, 1982) and explore, in a variety of settings,
those basic interpersonal ties and responsibilities[8] that tend to grow
within Alcoholics Anonymous.

APPENDIXES
NOTES
REFERENCES
INDEXES

APPENDIX A
THEORETICAL AND METHODOLOGICAL NOTES

M ETHODOLOGICAL techniques, like theoretical perspectives, are tools that shape, define, and focus research strategies. The methodological techniques utilized in studying the process of becoming alcoholic and the events leading to membership in A.A. were participant observation and in-depth interviewing in the form of topical life histories. These techniques are effective in understanding the world as the actor experiences it and are conducive to providing processual explanations of phenomena. In this appendix, I will discuss, first of all, general theoretical and methodological dimensions of the research strategy and, secondly, data analysis.

GENERAL THEORETICAL AND METHODOLOGICAL DIMENSIONS

Both the conception of deviance and social control underlying the present research as well as the theoretical underpinnings of participant observation and life histories draw heavily from a symbolic interactionist perspective. The symbolic interactionist perspective conceives humans as living in symbolic as well as physical environments, and it emphasizes that humans are stimulated to act by symbolic as well as by physical stimuli (Rose, 1962, p. 5). Stimuli, both physical and symbolic, are responded to in accordance with the definitions that actors give them (Stryker, 1964). Definitions or designations arise out of social interaction and are a product of one's own and others' definition of the situation (Blumer, 1969).

From the symbolic interactionist perspective, the individual is viewed as an aggressive actor (Blumer, 1969) or a self (Mead, 1934). According to Mead (1934), the self is a process and can best be viewed vis-à-vis two other subprocesses, the "I" and the "me." The "I" is the free or existential dimension of self. It is the acting self. "The 'me' is the organized set of attitudes of others" (Mead, 1934, p. 174). Of profound implication for self-concept and social control is the individual's ability to designate both himself or herself and others symbolically. Through these designations, the individual can "take the role of the other toward himself" (Mead, 1934, p. 254). Taking the attitudes of other individuals and the attitudes of the organized social group toward himself or herself allows the actor to be self-conscious as well as self-critical (Mead, 1934, p. 255). Role taking, because it allows the actor to anticipate cognitively (symbolically) the opinions and behavioral responses of others and to take these into account to modify or guide behavior, is the basis of social control. Social control of this type "refers not so much to deliberate influence or to coercion but to the fact that each person generally takes into account the expectations that he imputes to other people" (Shibutani, 1962, p. 129).

Briefly stated, the essential features of symbolic interactionism include symbols (primarily language), others, self, and interaction. Utilizing these elements, one would argue that drinking behavior can best be understood if we understand the symbolic and social matrix in which the self and others interact. From an interactionist perspective, the responses of individuals to alcohol and alcohol use are based on the definitions that they learn that pertain to alcohol and alcohol use. These definitions are the culmination of the individuals' interpretive and behavioral response to the definitions of others—both significant others and generalized others. Even the physiological concomitants of alcohol use are subject to the same interpretive process outlined above. I agree with MacAndrew and Edgerton (1969) that even drunken behavior is basically learned behavior and that it is learned in interaction with others.[1] Pharmacological properties of alcohol are less important in producing "alcohol experiences" than are perceptual and social factors. On the other hand, I believe an important and largely underemphasized research area is the effect of alcohol upon perception and, relatedly, the interplay between physiological and perceptual effects in producing drug-related experiences.

Because of the emphasis of symbolic interactionism on symbols, process, others, and interaction, methods that stress these features, as opposed to structural features, are a necessity. Participant observation and life-history interviewing fulfill these requirements in that they allow the researcher to enter into the world of subjects. This entry allows the researcher to maintain a firm grounding in the subjects' world so that he or she might understand their symbolizations and interactions and the meanings associated with them and, hence, their perception of the phenomena in question. Another advantage of observational methods, particularly in the sociology of deviance, is that the researcher is frequently cast in the role of the outsider. Since many deviants are, by definition, outsiders (Becker, 1963), such a situation allows the researcher to share the same type of status and, hopefully, to understand the actors' perspectives more fully.

Several researchers (Glaser and Strauss, 1965; Bruyn, 1966; Becker, 1970; Filstead, 1970; Schatzman and Strauss, 1973; Bogdan and Taylor, 1975; Schwartz and Jacobs, 1979; Shaffir et al., 1980) have recently written about the methods of participant observation. This technique of studying humans, as well as qualitative methods in general, allows the researcher to share in the life of the respondents and to see "what situations they meet and how they behave in them" (Becker, 1958, p. 652). Participant observation, when seen in this light, is more than simply an exploratory or descriptive strategy that is utilized prior to quantitative research. Rather, it is "a strategy concerned with the discovery of substantive theory"[2] (Glaser and Strauss, 1965, p. 6).

Prior to model or theory construction, there are two other distinct phases that occur in participant observation studies in the field. These include "the selection and definition of problems, concepts, and indices, and the check on the frequency and distribution of phenomena" (Becker, 1958, p. 653). The particulars of this research as they relate to these factors will be discussed shortly.

Life histories or case studies were more popular as a research strategy in the 1930s and 1940s than they are today (see Becker, 1966; Angell, 1945; and Park, 1952). Some of the best studies representative of this approach include Shaw's *The Jack-Roller* (1966), Lindesmith's study of opiate addiction (1947), and Lemert's research on check forgers (1958). As utilized in this research, life histories are extremely similar to participant observation. They differ only in the sense that they provide more detailed information, that the researcher has more control over the interactional sequence, and that only the experiences, definitions, interactional depictions, and meanings held by *one* person are gathered at a time. Like participant observation, the life history is particularly amenable to research emphasizing symbolic interactionism because a theory that stresses process and interaction and a theory "that stresses the 'subjective' side of social experience demands a methodology that explicitly focuses on such data" (Denzin, 1970), p. 258). Participant observation and life histories provide such methods.

The topical life histories were recorded and transcribed and ranged in time from one to eight hours. The interviews were unstructured but were similar in the way they were conducted and in the topics generally included. Interviews were formally initiated, that is, the tape recorder was turned on, after preliminary rapport building. These preliminaries included making coffee, making jokes, and "shooting the breeze" in order to make the respondents feel more comfortable. Once the tape recorder started, further rapport-building questions were asked. When I sensed that respondents had "settled in," I asked them to recall the events from initial drinking and childhood to the present, particularly as they thought these events related to their drinking careers. Additionally, the respondents were asked to recall how they thought about life events when they occurred and to point out if they felt differently about them now. From this point until near the termination of the interview, the only researcher-directed questions entailed elaboration and clarification. Simply stated, I listened to the respondents' life stories and expanded their data application by asking them about the how, why, and when, and about what it meant to them. When respondents realized that I was genuinely interested in hearing their views and not imposing my views on theirs, most of them became truly involved in telling their stories.[3]

Near the end of the interview, respondents were asked when and how they first perceived themselves as "alcoholics." Then, the respondents were asked if they wanted to add anything further. Additionally, they were asked if there was anything else that I should have asked them. Most respondents did not add anything, and with the three that chose to, the information tended to be a summary of their earlier comments. Interviews ended when no new or additional data resulted from a particular question or probe. To ensure that all pertinent areas were covered in the interviews, I developed a topical outline.

1. *Introduction.* I would like to get details about your story and your experience in your own words. Since I can't take shorthand and since I would really like to get everything, could I let this machine do the work? (Mention that interview is anonymous, use of pseudonyms for self, city, etc.). I'll ask you a few background questions, then maybe you could start telling me about your drinking career. One thing, though: when we get going, could you try and recall what happened and what you thought about it *then*? If you think differently about things now, could you explain how and why?

2. *Background Information and Rapport Building.* Ask about family background, religious background, length of time in program, occupation, and age. (I make an effort to get the respondents to relax by talking about our similarities. Also, I try not to make them feel that they are under a microscope.)

3. *Beliefs of Significant Others about Drinking.* What did parents and relatives think about alcohol usage? Explore drinking socialization. Explore alcoholic role models if they come up. When were you first aware of alcohol?

4. *Early Drinking Experiences and Their Repercussions.* First thought about drinking. Describe first drinking experience. How did you feel? What did you think about alcohol? How did significant others respond? Who else was involved? How did they feel?

5. *Elaboration of Drinking Career.* Also other careers—marital, occupational, etc. Emphasize what you thought about things. (I try to get the perspectives of significant others.) Did your drinking bother anybody?

6. *Feelings about Drinking.* Did you worry about your drinking? When? When did you think that your drinking was becoming a problem? What problems were related to your drinking? What seemed to bother you the most about your drinking? Important experiences relating to drinking or life in general. Ideas about alcoholism then and now. When did you regard yourself as an alcoholic? When did you accept it?

7. *Involvement with Labelers.* Probe for response of others. Explore involvement with social control agencies: hospitals, police, social workers, psychiatrists, and others.

8. *Alcoholics Anonymous.* Where did you learn about A.A.? A.A. socialization. Why did you come? What helped you make the program? What was tough about making it?

I used the outline as a guide for general topics. Some interviews progressed sequentially while others moved back and forth from the present to the past. Each interview was a specific interactional sequence in its own right and impressed upon me the importance that our biographies have for us.

Both interview and observational data were collected with an awareness of the major methodological problems typically encountered in field work. These pitfalls center around reactive effects of the observer's presence, distorting effects in perception and/or interpretation, and limitation to witness all relevant events (McCall, 1969). Reactive effects refer to biasing factors that might arise during an observational sequence because of the researcher's presence. Reactive effects may have been present during the early phases of the field research, particularly during casual conversations with individual members. However, with my access to closed meetings and acceptance that neared being regarded as a member, it is difficult to imagine reactive effects as significantly contributing to any bias in data collection. Additionally, reactive effects in general are overemphasized as a source of bias. Because participants in any setting have numerous social constraints and commitments, it is difficult for them to regard the researcher as the focal concern in interaction and to "tailor their behavior to what they think he might want or expect" (Becker, 1970, p. 47).

In terms of distorting effects of interpretation or selective perception, I strived to observe all that was occurring within various settings, avoided theoretically biasing questions, and searched for alternative definitions of the situation. These strategies prevented me from committing the errors of "going native" or being "ethnocentric" (Gold, 1958). In going native, researchers completely adopt the participants' definition of the situation and lose their objectivity in collecting data. Ethnocentrism refers to inserting one's own definition of the situation upon the participants and their interaction. Finally, biasing effects due to a failure to witness all relevant events were overcome by observing the members of A.A. in formal as well as informal aspects of the program. Members were observed during formal meetings when their focal concern was their alcoholism, and they were observed in informal settings when various other salient roles were emphasized.

DATA ANALYSIS

After I left the field, formal data analysis began.[4] Field notes and life histories were ordered chronologically and were read several times. These initial readings were utilized to search for coding categories. Categories ranged from descriptive to hypothetical in nature. For example, descriptive categories included the age and sex of A.A. members, the size of A.A. meetings attended, and various other attributes pertaining to the participants, the setting, and the interaction. Hypothetical categories included such items as members' definitions of alcoholism, members' self-descriptions, members' labeling, problems followed by alcoholism, alcoholism followed by problems. The tentative list of coding categories was thoroughly searched for redundancies and possible omissions. Once this was completed, each category was assigned a numerical value, and the field notes were reread and coded to follow this procedure.

It should be pointed out that a single datum can pertain to several of the coding categories. For example, a statement in the notes reads: "I became an alcoholic because I was such a superperfectionist." Categories pertinent to this statement include: "self-description or self-concept of member," "reason for alcoholism," and "defects of character." During the actual coding, when additional categories surfaced, they were added to the list and also coded.

The following is a listing of the coding categories utilized in summarizing and analyzing field notes. Some categories are obviously descriptive while others are hypothetical. To give the reader a better feel for this coding scheme, several pages of coded field notes will follow the listing of the coded categories.

Coding Categories

RESEARCHER-SUBJECT RELATIONSHIP

1. Rapport
2. Researcher role
3. Researcher as alcoholic

ORGANIZATIONAL ASPECTS

4. Meeting location
5. Meeting composition
6. Group structure
7. Organizational slogans
8. Realization of the program
9. A.A. as a "greedy organization"
10. "A.A. as a way of life"
11. Relationship between A.A. and other agencies

PERSONAL ATTRIBUTES OF MEMBERS

12. Marital status
13. Age
14. Gender
15. Race
16. Social class
17. Education
18. Occupation

BECOMING AN A.A. MEMBER

19. Finding out about A.A.
20. Making A.A. contacts
21. Dramatic incidents leading to A.A.
22. God and miracles
23. Reasons for joining
24. Reasons for staying

BECOMING AN ALCOHOLIC

25. First drinking experience
26. First drunk
27. Self-perception or self-concept
28. Frequency of drinking

29. Quantity of drinking
30. Location of drinking
31. Drinking companions
32. Drinking behavior
33. Sneaking drinks
34. Morning drinks
35. Reasons for drinking
36. Blackouts
37. Loss of control
38. Benders
39. Guilt
40. Other drugs
41. Regulation of drinking
42. Quitting
43. Testing the cure
44. Alcoholic role models

CAREER CONTINGENCIES

45. Loss of friends (also threatened losses)
46. Loss of family (also threatened losses)
47. Loss of job (also threatened losses)
48. Arguments with significant others over drinking
49. Physical problems
50. Legal problems
51. Suicide
52. Other contingencies (wife is abstainer, violent temper, job requires drinking, etc.)

DEFINITIONS

53. Define drinking as problem
54. Define drinking as result of problem
55. Define self as alcoholic
56. Others define self as alcoholic
57. Definitions of alcoholism
58. Define self as A.A.
59. Reasons for alcoholism

OTHERS (THE FOLLOWING CATEGORIES WERE ADDED DURING THE CODING.)

60. Dry drunks
61. Anonymity
62. Reference individual in self-definition of alcoholic

63. Alcoholic stereotype as rationalization for drinking
64. "Conning"
65. "Alcoholic thinking"
66. Early responsibility forced upon individual
67. "Insanity"
68. Personal failures
69. Relief from drinking
70. Relief at A.A.
71. Occupational rationalization—if I have a job I can't be an alcoholic
72. Alcoholic careers vs. mentally ill careers
73. Addictive personality
74. Length of drinking career
75. Hangovers

September 28, 1973—Middle Group
Excerpt from Testimonial

My name is Carl, and I am an alcoholic. I've never   14
spoken at this meeting before, and I'm glad to be here.
My drinking career started at age seventeen. In my own
mind, I think that if alcohol had not gotten me, some-   25
thing else would have. Anyway you look at it, I think I
would have had problems. My hang-up was that I had an
inferiority complex. I was a good student in high school,   27, 35
but I just felt inferior.   27

After I graduated, I got a job in SC, where a large elec-
trical engineering company was located. I didn't have any   18
problems there, but I was drinking more. Just like before,
every time I drank I got drunk. There was no compulsion
to drink, but once I got started I always tried to do a good   32
job. I guess one of the reasons I didn't get into any trouble   37
in SC is because I was only there for six months. After   52
that, I was transferred to UT, where the company also
had a plant. In UT, I really felt alone. I didn't have any
friends or relatives around, so I think it was just natural
for me to get into booze a little more. During this time,
I became friends with another guy who was also a bach-   52
elor, and we got an apartment together. I think the com-   31
pany did me a lot of good. Unfortunately, he liked to
drink also, and I don't think that helped me much. We
used to have beer every night at supper and drink most of   32
the evening also. At the time, I guess I just thought it was
a bad habit, but pretty soon the habit turned into a need.   35

I continued to drink more often and in larger quanti-   32
ties. A day didn't go by that I didn't have a drink. However, I never had any problems at work either. I always   28
showed up and did my job. Hangovers weren't a problem   52
because if you don't get sober you won't get a hangover.
As a matter of fact I don't think I ever got sick or had   75
more than a little hangover during my last eight years of
drinking. My habit of drinking in the morning probably   34
helped me out though.   69
Early in the 1960s, drinking was taking over my life   37
totally. I wasn't really aware of it then, but looking back
on it now, I know that's the way I feel. I didn't even have
any inferiority complex any more. The truth of the mat-   69
ter was that I was too drunk to know if I had an inferiority   32
complex or not. I used to talk with people, crack jokes,   69
and even do a little dancing when I was in the world of
booze.
I don't exactly remember when or how, but I ended up
at an A.A. meeting one day. I couldn't identify with anything that was going on. Those things that everybody was   20
talking about never happened to me. I wasn't divorced. I   52
never tried to kill myself. I was a college graduate. I had
never been fired. Anyway, since A.A. had nothing for   18
me, I didn't stick around.   71

Once the notes were coded, a large matrix was constructed, show-
ing a frequency distribution of the coded categories on each page of
the field notes. This procedure enabled me to glance at the matrix
and determine how frequently an event occurred and what other
events occurred with it. Additionally, the matrix provided an index
for use during the writing stages of this manuscript. For example,
when I wrote the organization chapter, I located the pertinent categories in the matrix. It was then a simple matter of referring to the
pages listed where one could best find information relating to the
organizational aspects in question. This procedure was followed in
ferreting out information pertaining to the research questions. Additionally, many hours were spent examining the matrix and searching out other possible themes and findings.

To establish the worth of any evidence bearing on the support or
negation of hypotheses and themes, procedures suggested in the
qualitative research literature were utilized. Evidence was categorized according to whether the informants were credible, whether

the evidence was reported to the researcher alone or took place
within the group, and whether it was volunteered or directed (Becker
and Geer, 1960). Other important dimensions that field researchers
must take into account include the proportion of respondents who
support a given hypothesis, the accountability of any negative evidence, and the kind of person (researcher or respondent) providing
the inference necessary to connect events (Becker, 1958). Each of
the items mentioned above was checked against all findings so that
evidence contamination and its effects could be controlled.[5]

APPENDIX B
A.A. MEMBERSHIP

B ECAUSE A.A. has never attempted to keep formal membership lists, it is extremely difficult to obtain accurate figures on total membership at any given time. Some local groups are not registered with the General Service Office. Others do not estimate membership on the registration data cards filed there. The membership figures listed below are based on reports to the General Office as of January 1984, plus an average allowance for groups that have not reported their membership.

There is no practical way of counting members who are not affiliated with a local group.

A.A. Membership and Group Information

Groups in U.S.	29,827
Members in U.S.	585,823
Groups in Canada	4,197

Members in Canada	69,931
Groups Overseas	22,156
Members Overseas	466,897
Internationalists	522
Groups in Treatment Facilities (U.S./Canada)	1,052
Members in Treatment Facilities (U.S./Canada)	25,899
Groups in Correctional Facilities (U.S./Canada	1,344
Members in Correctional Facilities (U.S./Canada	42,336
Lone Members	508

Total Reported

1,191,946 Members
58,576 Groups

Adapted from the A.A. Fact File (1984).

NOTES

1. Perspectives on Alcoholics Anonymous

1. Rather than explicitly developing the research literature on A.A. in a literature review section, I will employ a strategy suggested in qualitative research (Bogdan and Taylor, 1975) of integrating and discussing research where it most closely relates with my argument. For the most inclusive listing of A.A. citations and an overview of A.A., the reader should examine Leach (1973), Leach and Norris (1977), and Kurtz (1979). For other ethnographic accounts of A.A. consult Gellman (1964), Madsen (1974), Robinson (1979), and Maxwell, (1984).

2. More than ten years have passed since I left the field. However, the freshness of these data is of less importance than their validity. Over the years, A.A. friends and A.A. members who listened to papers presented or read articles I published have nearly unanimously accepted my interpretations. Recent books (Robinson, 1979; Maxwell, 1984) and dissertations (Taylor, 1977; Chaiken, 1979) on A.A. in different settings do not contradict what I develop here. An additional validity check results from referees' comments on this

book and on other journal articles describing these data. Nearly half of the reviews that addressed my relationship to A.A. charged that I have gone "native" while the other half argued that I have been superficial or ethnocentric. I interpret such disagreement as support that I have successfully straddled the middle of the road.

3. At my third closed meeting (weekenders group), a middle-aged male, Herb, passed on his discussion turn by saying, "I have some resentments. I probably shouldn't, but I don't feel like sharing anything tonight." I felt that his "resentments" were due to my presence, but I was too unsure of myself to ask. Three months later, after we got to know each other better, Herb brought up that first meeting. He admitted that my presence had bothered him that night. Because of this experience and worries about intrusion, I concentrated on closed-group observations at the weekenders' group and the late night group. Both groups had small attendance (6 to 15), and I had good rapport with nearly all the members.

4. Just when I felt "accepted" in the field, an experience occurred that questioned my empathy skills: As I was leaving the open house, I saw two couples around my age exit the bar next door and "stumble" toward the open house. One of the men shouted, "Hey, maybe we should try some of that A.A. stuff!" The others screamed in agreement and headed directly toward me. I heard one of the women say, "There's one of them now, right there." Before they turned and walked away, we briefly looked at each other. The words were forming on my lips, "But I'm not really one of them, I'm just . . ."

5. There are approximately three males to every female in Mid-eastern City A.A. Females tended to cluster at meetings in small groups of three to five and were less integrated into the group as a whole. Additionally, at many of the informal meetings where rapport was being established for life-history interviews, females were absent. Accordingly, I felt that females should be excluded from the life histories. However, females are at least proportionately represented in the testimonial data.

6. For a more detailed treatment of the history of A.A. see *Alcoholics Anonymous Comes of Age* (1957) and *Not God: A History of Alcoholics Anonymous* (Kurtz, 1979).

7. A.A. *Comes of Age* (1957) reports Washingtonian membership at 500,000 (p. 125). However, Sagarin argues that even his lower figure is probably subject to inflation.

8. Bill W.'s involvement with the Oxford Groups and Dr. Bob's medical training are the central ideological bases for A.A. The medical-moral ideological base that evolved is described in Siegler et al. (1968).

9. See Kurtz (1979) for an informative discussion of the organizational and political dynamics behind Bill Wilson's introduction of the Twelve Traditions.

10. This is the procedure of the middle group. Some groups have longer chairing periods, but one year is probably the maximum.

11. Greedy organizations, by definition, keep people busy. Wiseman (1972) suggests that time is an alcoholic's worst enemy. The likelihood of "staying sober a day at a time" is increased in greedy organizations because they demand so much of their individuals' time resources.

2. The Process of Affiliation with A.A.

1. This chapter was written in collaboration with Arthur Greil. A similar version appeared in *Qualitative Sociology* 6 (1983): 5–20. Reprinted by permission.

2. The word "reputation" is used because objective, quantifiable data on A.A. success are meager in that little systematic research has been undertaken. For a summary of existing studies see Leach (1973) and Leach and Norris (1977).

3. Dissertations by Taylor (1977) and Chaiken (1979) as well as Maxwell's research (1984) provide excellent additional material on some of these phases. Taylor's work particularly is useful because she casts A.A. resocialization along lines of identity transformation and because she highlights several writers in the conversion literature not emphasized in this chapter. Bateson's work (1971) is also important because it examines conversion on a deeper philosophical level. Specifically, he views conversion in A.A. as the result of the alcoholic spiritually rejecting an epistemology of pride, control, dominance, and centrality for an epistemology that is directed outward toward others. Recognizing one's vulnerability, dependence, and relatedness to others and to the larger world are characteristics of this new epistemology.

4. Several factors—increased funding, the inception of the National Institute on Alcohol Abuse and Alcoholism (NIAAA), and the 1976 Federal Comprehensive Alcohol Abuse, Prevention, Treat-

ment and Rehabilitation Act—have expanded the number and types of agencies that encourage, refer, or force persons to make contact with A.A. Room (1982) discusses other contemporary changes in the social control of alcohol problems.

5. My meaning of "first stepping" here is somewhat different from the meaning that most A.A. members stress. Rather than emphasizing "surrender," at the emotional or "gut level," I am emphasizing a behavioral and intellectual awareness in beginning or taking the first step in A.A. For a more phenomenological interpretation of "surrender" and the "first step" see Tiebout (1949, 1961), Bateson (1971), Kurtz (1979), and Anderson (1982).

6. Frequently, "Is A.A. for you?" a brief pamphlet and questionnaire, is given to the newcomer.

7. Officially, there are no formal ties between Alanon, Alateen, and A.A. However, the families of A.A. members are typically referred to these organizations, and in Mideastern City some A.A. groups meet at the same time and in the same building as Alanon meetings.

8. Although many Mideastern City A.A. members complete twelfth-step calls prior to story telling, they usually do it as the second member of a team. Twelfth-step work continues more consistently after the affiliate has told his or her story, and it is one of the most frequently occurring and most important of all A.A. activities.

3. Explanations and Their Functions

1. Two points must be clarified here. First, I do not argue that self-definitions do not undergo change in A.A. but rather that individuals, in utilizing disease definitions, can start the A.A. program with the belief that the solution to their alcoholism is in not drinking as opposed to changing their personality. Second, some individuals, both within and outside of A.A., have utilized explanations that diminish personal responsibility not to achieve sobriety but to justify further drinking (Roman and Trice, 1968).

2. Maxwell (1984, pp. 17–38) provides explanations of members that are similar to those described in this chapter.

4. A Typology of Careers

1. These data can not be viewed in rigid variable terms; rather, I am applying some measurement to better describe sensitizing concepts.

2. These other sources were useful because some old-timers with heavy drinking emphasis careers tended to tell sobriety stories during story telling.

3. Alcohol counselors and the like might argue that the individuals who reject A.A. at this time are engaging in rationalization. There is no way of determining if this is the case. Furthermore, the term "rationalization" is a severe value judgment because it results from a therapist's or clinician's decision that his or her perspective of reality is correct while the patient's is false. The opposite notion is rarely considered.

4. The question of how and when primary deviance becomes secondary deviance is extremely important on the empirical as well as the theoretical level. These data offer no clear-cut solution but suggest that the shift can be sudden and dramatic, or gradual and routine, and that the shift involves the drinker's meanings as well as the meanings of others in the situation.

5. Psychologically, these individuals might be considered as typical alcoholics rationalizing their behavior or being deluded by a discrepancy between true and false selves. Lemert (1972) entertains the false self-idea and borrows the concept from R. D. Laing (1965). However, sociologically, one should be extremely careful of schemes viewing outsiders' perceptions of an actor's self-concept as being more correct than the actor's perception. From a symbolic interactionalist approach, one must never lose sight of the fact that there are several perspectives regarding the definition of any object in all interactional sequences.

6. This account raises some important issues, particularly the element of passing as "normal" in a social situation. Without further questioning, it is impossible to determine if the respondent really had a compulsion to drink or developed the feeling because of the fear of being caught at passing.

7. Converted alcoholics, like other alcoholics, sometimes approach A.A. on more than one occasion before affiliating. Limited discussion of this point for converted and tangential alcoholics is due to the relatively low frequency of these categories. Additionally, these findings must be treated carefully because one does not know the number of individuals in any alcoholic career that approach the organization, leave, and never return.

8. It becomes difficult and meaningless to state the average length

of alcoholic careers for converted and tangential alcoholics because of the lack of emphasis that they give to drinking.

9. Also, there is no statement regarding a connection between drinking and behavior. Accordingly, this is indirect evidence or support for our interpretation.

10. I am not saying that tangential alcoholics are necessarily passing, but I considered passing as a possibility and was careful in questioning them.

5. Slipping and Sobriety

1. A briefer and different version of this chapter appeared in the *Journal of Studies on Alcohol* 41 (July, 1980): 727–32. Reprinted by permission.

2. In the Edwards et al. research (1966, 1967), the percentage of slippers is probably higher than reported because newcomers were excluded from their analysis. Newcomers tend to have high slipping rates (Bailey and Leach, 1965; Alcoholics Anonymous, 1970).

3. A similar point was later made by George Herbert Mead (1918).

4. These behaviors and the norms they exemplify are not exhaustive of all A.A. norms. Gellman (1964) presents an excellent discussion of the normative structure of A.A.

5. According to A.A., the only requirement for membership is a desire to stop drinking, so technically slippers are still considered group members. However, sociologically, they qualify as nonmembers or deviant members. Aspects of this role include being submissive, keeping quiet if still under the influence, confessing to the group, etc.

6. Gellman (1964) is one of the few researchers who point out that the response to slipping in A.A., namely sympathy and understanding, enhances group solidarity.

7. Norman Denzin has suggested to me that in some situations and contexts slipping could be devastating and damaging to group morale. Although I never encountered such an occurrence, I strongly believe that it is more than a remote possibility. As Coser (1962) has demonstrated, group responses to deviance and the ultimate structural outcomes are variables in their own right, so logically a group could be strengthened or weakened by deviance.

6. THE CONSTRUCTION OF ALCOHOLISM: A.A. AND JELLINEK'S PHASE MODEL

1. Jellinek distinguishes between "alcoholic addicts" and "habitual symptomatic drinkers": "In both groups the excessive drinking is symptomatic of underlying psychological or social pathology, but in one group after several years of excessive drinking 'loss of control' over the alcohol intake occurs, while in the other group this phenomenon never develops. The group with the loss of control is designated as 'alcohol addicts'" (Jellinek, 1962, p. 357).

2. Jellinek actually cautioned about this difficulty in the data, but both his presentations (1946, 1952) were written in a manner that depicted and strongly suggested ordering. For example, he writes that "the sequences of symptoms within the phases are characteristic, however, of the great majority of alcohol addicts and represent what may be called the average trend" (Jellinek, 1952).

3. Respondents were asked at what age they first experienced a blackout. This was followed by an example that entailed waking up the next day and forgetting events pertaining to the previous night. Accordingly, as Goodwin et al. (1969) note, blackouts could not really be distinguished from possible amnesia.

4. Room (1978) argues in his dissertation that Jellinek's phase model was widely accepted and received little criticism because it fulfilled a need in elaborating a specific model of disease (p. 64). More importantly, he describes links between various organizational realms and alcohologists like E. M. Jellinek and Selden Bacon from a broader personal, social, and political perspective (1978, pp. 108–47). Room's involvement in alcohol research, funding, and policy making has accorded him a broad view shared by only a few sociologists in the alcohol field.

5. There are some members who specifically deny blackouts. They are usually held as the exception that proves the rule.

7. AN INTERACTIONIST DEFINITION OF ALCOHOLISM

1. Tournier (1979) illustrates the dominance of A.A. ideology in contemporary alcoholism treatment and argues that the organization has "fettered innovation," "precluded early intervention," and "limited treatment strategies" (pp. 230–31). I agree with this to a point but feel that many A.A. members are becoming increasingly accepting of alternative treatment modalities and alcoholism mod-

els. The increase of "high-bottom" alcoholics in A.A. and the A.A. slogan "Live and let live," coupled with the organization's maturity, are factors related to increased tolerance.

2. Clearly, the term "strange" is relativistic, and relativism is strongly intended and will be discussed later in this chapter.

3. Even the "Big Book," *Alcoholics Anonymous* (1955), illustrates this point. Inside the jacket flap is the following: "If you wish to preserve complete personal anonymity when carrying this book, just turn the jacket inside out. It has been especially designed for your convenience."

4. My overemphasis on perceptual, social, and cultural effects may be a slight overreaction to the long-term overemphasis upon the pharmacological properties of alcohol. The view emphasized throughout this research is that perceptual/definitional realities mesh with physiological ones. Alcohol is one of the most destructive drugs widely used in American society. Its organically destructive properties are well known. Many A.A. members, during their drinking careers, oriented their entire lives around the ingestion of alcohol. However, to implicate only the drug and human physiology oversimplifies and distorts the lives and experiences of many heavy drinkers as well as research data within contemporary alcohology.

5. My observations within A.A. would support Scheff's argument (1966). Frequently, A.A. members told newcomers that "any drinking could be alcoholism." Additionally, experience has illustrated that virtually anyone who approached A.A. would be typed an "alcoholic."

8. ALCOHOLIC WORLDS AND SOCIOLOGICAL WORLDS

1. For a more typical and detailed account of the sociological literature on alcoholism see Rudy (1977) and White (1982).

2. Glassner and Berg's recent work (1984) demonstrates how social structure shapes American Jews' interpretation of alcoholism.

3. From the perspective of A.A., an alcoholic is one whose life has become unmanageable bcause of alcohol. Relatively and symbolically speaking, alcoholics are those who regard themselves as such.

4. The Rand Report (Armor et al., 1976) and its follow-up (Polich et al., 1980a, 1980b) sparked major responses from total abstinence

proponents and others. The interested reader is referred to the following sources: Armor et al. (1978) and Heather and Robertson (1981).

5. Because of methodological differences, the objective reader cannot resolve this debate through perusal of the published studies. Goode (1984) and Akers (1985) reached a similar conclusion.

6. See Room (1976, 1978) for criticism and discussion of "ambivalence" as a governing image of sociological views on alcoholism.

7. Recent work (Mulford and Fitzgerald, 1983a; 1983b; Fitzgerald and Mulford, 1984) questions simple correlations between average per capita consumption and problem drinking. See Frankel and Whitehead (1981) for a discussion and theoretical elaboration of the "alcohol consumption and damage" literature.

8. "Constructive confrontation" between supervisors and employees is a successful strategy in employee assistance programs (Trice and Beyer, 1982). Expansion of such strategies into other settings needs to be explored.

APPENDIX A:
THEORETICAL AND METHODOLOGICAL NOTES

1. Becker (1963, 1967) presents other classic research documenting how physiological properties of drugs are subject to interpretations developed through interactional sequences.

2. By "substantive theory" Glaser and Strauss mean "the formulation of concepts and their interrelations into a set of hypotheses for a given substantive behavior—such as patient care, gang behavior, or education, based on research in the area" (1965, p. 6).

3. One eight-hour interview turned into inventory taking (A.A. step 5). The only "bad" interview involved a college professor who kept asking me what I really wanted to know.

4. In participant observation, research data collection and analysis are not distinct phases. Initial data analysis takes place during data collection in that the observer's comments represent emerging hypotheses or general descriptive themes. For an excellent discussion of this point see Glaser and Strauss (1965, pp. 289–92).

5. In addition to Becker (1958), other accountability schemes useful in determining data contamination include Bell (1965), Bruyn (1966), Glaser and Strauss (1967), and Vidich (1955).

REFERENCES

AKERS, R.
  1977   *Deviant Behavior: A Social Learning Approach.* Bel-
  1985   mont, CA: Wadsworth Publishing.

ALBRECHT, G.
  1973   "The Alcoholism Process: A Social Learning View-
          point." In *Alcoholism: Progress in Research and Treat-
          ment,* edited by P. Bourne and R. Fox, 11–34. New
          York: The Academic Press.

ALCOHOLICS ANONYMOUS
  1939   *Alcoholics Anonymous: The Story of How Many Thou-
  1955   sands of Men and Women Have Recovered from Alco-
  1976   holism.* New York: Alcoholics Anonymous World Ser-
          vices.

  1953   *Twelve Steps and Twelve Traditions.* New York: Alcohol-
          ics Anonymous Publishing.

  1957   *Alcoholics Anonymous Comes of Age: A Brief History of
          A.A.* New York: Alcoholics Anonymous Publishing.

ALEXANDER, J.
  1941   "Alcoholics Anonymous: Freed Slaves of Drink, Now
          They Free Others." *Saturday Evening Post* 219:9–11.

ANDERSON, D.
  1982   "A.A. and the Growing Self-Help Movement." In *Alco-
          holism: Analysis of a World-Wide Problem*, edited by
          P. Golding, 221–29. Lancaster, England: MTP Press.

ANGELL, R.
  1945   "The Use of Personal Documents in History, Anthropol-
          ogy, and Sociology." Social Science Research Council:
          Bulletin 53.

ARMOR, D., J. POLICH, AND H. STAMBUL
  1976   *Alcoholism and Treatment.* Santa Monica, CA: Rand
          Corporation.
  1978   *Alcoholism and Treatment.* New York: Wiley.

BACON, S. D.
  1945   *Inebriety, Social Integration, and Marriage.* New Haven:
          Yale Univ. Pr.
  1962   "Alcohol and Complex Society." In *Society, Culture, and
          Drinking Patterns*, edited by D. J. Pittman and C. R.
          Snyder, 78–84. New York: John Wiley.
  1973   "The Process of Addiction to Alcohol." *Quarterly Jour-
          nal of Studies on Alcohol* 34:1–27.

BAILEY, M. B., AND B. LEACH
  1965   *Alcoholics Anonymous: Pathway to Recovery.* New York:
          National Council on Alcoholism.

BALES, R. F.
  1945   "Social Therapy for a Social Disorder—Compulsive
          Drinking." *Journal of Social Issues* 1:14–22.
  1949   "Cultural Differences in Rates of Alcoholism." *Quarterly
          Journal of Studies on Alcohol* 6:480–99.

BATESON, G.
  1971   "The Cybernetics of 'Self': A Theory of Alcoholism."
          Psychiatry 34:1–18.

BEAUCHAMP, D.
  1980   *Beyond Alcoholism: Alcohol and Public Health Policy.*
          Philadelphia: Temple Univ. Pr.

BECKER, H. S.
  1953   "Becoming a Marihuana User." *American Journal of So-
          ciology* 59:235–42.

1958   "Problems of Inference and Proof in Participant Obser-
        vation." *American Sociological Review* 23:652–60.
1960   "Notes on the Concept of Commitment." *American
        Journal of Sociology* 66:32–40.
1963   *Outsiders: Studies in the Sociology of Deviance.* New
1973   York: The Free Press of Glencoe.
1966   Introduction to *The Jack-Roller,* by C. Shaw. Chicago:
        Univ. of Chicago Pr.
1967   "History, Culture, and Subjective Experience: An Explo-
        ration of the Social Bases of Drug-Induced Experi-
        ences." *Journal of Health and Social Behavior* 8:163–
        76.
1970   *Sociological Work: Method and Substance.* Chicago: Al-
        dine Publishing.

BECKER, H. S., AND B. GEER
1960   "Participant Observation: The Analysis of Qualitative
        Field Data." In *Human Organization Research,* edited
        by R. Adams and J. Reiss, 267–89. Homewood, IL:
        Dorsey Press.

BERGER, P., AND T. LUCKMAN
1966   *The Social Construction of Reality.* New York: Double-
        day and Company.

BIERSTEDT, R.
1959   "Nominal and Real Definitions in Sociological Theory."
        In *Symposium on Sociological Theory,* edited by L.
        Gross, 121–44. Evanston, IL: Row, Peterson and
        Company.

BIGUS, O.
1974   "Becoming 'Alcoholic'! A Study of Social Transforma-
        tion." Ph.D. diss., Univ. of California, San Francisco.

BLANE, H. T., AND L. E. HEWITT
1977   *Alcohol and Youth: An Analysis of the Literature, 1960–
        1975.* Pittsburgh: The Univ. of Pennsylvania.

BLUMBERG, L.
1977   "The Ideology of a Therapeutic Social Movement: Al-
        coholics Anonymous." *Journal of Studies on Alcohol*
        38:2122–43.

BLUMER, H.
1969   *Symbolic Interactionism.* Englewood Cliffs, NJ: Prentice
        Hall.

BOGDAN, R., AND S. TAYLOR
1975   *Introduction to Qualitative Research Methods: A Phenomenological Approach to the Social Sciences.* New York: John Wiley and Sons.

BOHINCE, E., AND A. ORENSTEEN
1950   "An Evaluation of the Services and Programs of the Minneapolis Chapter of Alcoholics Anonymous." Master's thesis, Univ. of Minnesota.

BOSCARINO, J.
1980   "Factors Related to 'Stable' and 'Unstable' Affiliation with Alcoholics Anonymous." *The International Journal of the Addictions* 15:839–44.

BOURNE, P., AND R. FOX
1973   *Alcoholism: Progress in Research and Treatment.* New York: The Academic Press.

BROWN, M. A.
1950   "Alcoholic Profiles on the Minnesota Multiphasic." *Journal of Clinical and Experimental Psychology* 6:266–69.

BRUYN, S.
1966   *The Human Perspective in Sociology: The Methodology of Participant Observation.* Englewood Cliffs, NJ: Prentice Hall.

BUNZEL, R.
1940   "The Role of Alcoholism in Two Central American Cultures." *Psychiatry* 3:361–87.

BUTTON, A. D.
1956   "Psychodynamics of Alcoholism." *Quarterly Journal of Studies on Alcohol* 17:456.

C., BILL
1965   "The Growth and Effectiveness of Alcoholics Anonymous in a Southwestern City." *Quarterly Journal of Studies on Alcohol* 26:279–84.

CADDY, G., H. ADDINGTON, AND D. PERKINS
1978   "Individualized Behavior Therapy for Alcoholics: A Third-Year Independent Double-Blind Follow-up." *Behavioral Research and Therapy* 16:345–62.

CAHALAN, D.
1970   *Problem Drinkers: A National Survey.* San Francisco: Jossey Bass.

1978   "Implications of American Drinking Practices and Attitudes for Prevention and Treatment of Alcoholism." In *Behavioral Approaches to Alcoholism*, edited by G. G. Marlatt and P. Nathan, 6–26. New Brunswick, NJ: Rutgers Center of Alcohol Studies.

CAHALAN, D., I. H. CISIN, AND H. M. CROSSLEY
1969   *American Drinking Practices*. New Brunswick, NJ.: Rutgers Center of Alcohol Studies.

CAHALAN, D., AND R. ROOM
1974   *Problem Drinking Among American Men*. New Haven, CT: College and Univ. Pr.

CANTER, T.
1966   "Personality Factors Related to Participation in Treatment of Hospitalized Male Alcoholics." *Journal of Clinical Psychology* 22:114–16.

CANTRIL, H.
1963   *The Psychology of Social Movements*. New York: Wiley.

CHAIKEN, M.
1979   "Alcoholics Anonymous: A Sociological Study." Ph.D. diss., Univ. of California, Los Angeles.

CHAMBERS, F. T.
1953   "Analysis and Comparison of Three Treatment Measures for Alcoholism: Antabuse, the Alcoholics Anonymous Approach, and Psychotherapy." *British Journal of Addiction* 50:29–41.

CHANDLER, JR., C. HENSMAN, AND G. EDWARDS
1971   "Determinants of What Happens to Alcoholics." *Quarterly Journal of Studies on Alcohol* 32:349–63.

CLANCY, J.
1964   "Motivational Conflicts of the Alcohol Addict." *Quarterly Journal of Studies on Alcohol* 25:511–20.

CLARK, W., AND D. CAHALAN
1976   "Changes in Problem Drinking over a Four-Year Span." *Addictive Behaviors* 1:251–60.

CONGER, J.
1956   "Reinforcement Theory and the Dynamics of Alcoholism." *Quarterly Journal of Studies on Alcohol* 17:296–305.

1958   "Perception, Learning, and Emotion: The Role of Alcohol." *Annals* 315: 31–39.

CONRAD, P.
1975   "The Discovery of Hyperkinesis: Notes on the Medicalization of Deviant Behavior." *Social Problems* 23:12–21.
1976   "Towards a Theory of the Medicalization of Deviance." Paper presented at the annual meeting of the Society for the Study of Social Problems, New York.

CONRAD, P., AND J. SCHNEIDER
1980   *Deviance and Medicalization.* St. Louis: C. V. Mosby.

CORDER, B. F., A. HENDRICKS, AND R. F. CORDER
1964   "An MMPI Study of a Group of Wives of Alcoholics." *Quarterly Journal of Studies on Alcohol* 34:409–13.

COSER, L.
1962   "Some Functions of Deviant Behavior and Normative Flexibility." *American Journal of Sociology* 68:172–81.
1967   "Greedy Organizations." *European Journal of Sociology* 8:196–215.

CURLEE, J.
1973   "Alcoholic Blackouts: Some Conflicting Evidence." *Quarterly Journal of Studies on Alcohol* 34:409–13.

CURLEE-SALISBURY, J.
1982   "Perspectives on Alcoholics Anonymous." In *Alcoholism: Development, Consequences, and Interventions,* edited by N. Estes and M. Heinemann, 311–18. St. Louis: C. V. Mosby.

DAVIES, D.
1962   "Normal Drinking in Recovered Alcohol Addicts." *Quarterly Journal of Studies on Alcohol* 23:94–104.

DAVIS, F.
1961   "Deviance Disavowal: The Management of Strained Interaction by the Visibly Handicapped." *Social Problems* 9:120–32.

DENZIN, N.
1970   *The Research Act: A Theoretical Introduction to Sociological Methods.* Chicago: Aldine Publishing.

DURKHEIM, E.
1938   *The Rules of Sociological Method.* Glencoe, IL: The Free Press.

EDWARDS, G., C. HENSMAN, A. HAWKER, AND V. WILLIAMSON
1966   "Who Goes to Alcoholics Anonymous?" *Lancet* 11:382–84.
1967   "Alcoholics Anonymous: The Anatomy of a Self-Help Group." *Social Psychiatry* 1:195–204.

EDWARDS, G., E. KYLE, AND P. NICHOLLS
1974   "Alcoholics Admitted to Four England Hospitals." *Quarterly Journal of Studies on Alcohol* 35:499–522.

EMRICK, C. D.
1974   "A Review of Psychologically Oriented Treatment of Alcoholism." *Quarterly Journal of Studies on Alcohol* 35:523–49.

ERIKSON, K. T.
1966   *Wayward Puritans.* New York: John Wiley and Sons.

FIELD, P. B.
1962   "A New Cross-Cultural Study of Drunkenness." In *Society, Culture, and Drinking Patterns*, edited by D. J. Pittman and C. R. Snyder, 48–74. New York: Wiley.

FILSTEAD, W.
1970   *Qualitative Methodology: Firsthand Involvement with the Social World.* Chicago: Markham Publishing.

FITZGERALD, J., AND H. MULFORD
1984   "Seasonal Changes in Alcohol Consumption and Related Problems in Iowa, 1979–1980." *Journal of Studies on Alcohol* 45:363–68.

FRANKEL, B. G., AND P. WHITEHEAD
1981   *Drinking and Damage: Theoretical Advances and Implications for Prevention.* New Brunswick, NJ: Rutgers Center of Alcohol Studies.

FREIDSON, E.
1966   "Disability as Social Deviance." In *Scoiology and Rehabilitation*, edited by M. B. Sussman, 71–99. Washington: U.S. Department of Health, Education and Welfare.

GARFINKEL, H.
1967   *Studies in Ethnomethodology.* Englewood Cliffs, NJ: Prentice Hall.

GELLMAN, I. P.
1964   *The Sober Alcoholic: An Organizational Analysis of Alcoholics Anonymous.* New Haven, CT: College and Univ. Pr.

GERLACH, L. P., AND V. HINE
1968   "Five Factors Crucial to the Growth and Spread of a Modern Religious Movement." *Journal for the Scientific Study of Religion* 7:23–40.

GLASER, B., AND A. STRAUSS
1965   "The Discovery of Substantive Theory: A Basic Strategy Underlying Qualitative Research." *The American Behavioral Scientist* 8:5–12.
1967   *The Discovery of Grounded Theory: Strategies for Qualitative Research.* Chicago: Aldine Publishing.
1970   "The Discovery of Substantive Theory." In *Qualitative Methodology,* edited by W. Filstead, 288–304. Chicago: Markham.

GLASSNER, B., AND B. BERG
1980   "How Jews Avoid Alcohol Problems." *American Sociological Review* 45:647–64.
1984   "Social Locations and Interpretations: How Jews Define Alcoholism." *Journal of Studies on Alcohol* 45:16–25.

GLATT, M. M.
1970   *The Alcoholic and the Help He Needs.* London: Priority Press.

GOFFMAN, E.
1961   *Asylums.* Garden City, NY: Anchor Books.
1963   *Stigma: Notes on the Management of Spoiled Identity.* Englewood Cliffs, NJ: Prentice Hall.

GOLD, R.
1958   "Roles in Sociological Field Observations." *Social Forces* 36:217–23.

GOODE, E.
1972   *Drugs in American Society.* New York: Knopf.
1984
1978   *Deviant Behavior: An Interactionist Approach.* Englewood Cliffs, NJ: Prentice Hall.

GOODWIN, D., B. CRANE, AND S. GUZE
1969   "Alcoholic Blackouts: A Review and Clinical Study of 100 Alcoholics." *American Journal of Psychiatry* 126:191–98.

GREIL, A. L., AND D. R. RUDY
   1984   "Sociological Cocoons: Encapsulation and Identity
           Change Organizations." *Sociological Inquiry* 54:260–
           78.

GUSFIELD, J.
   1963   *Symbolic Crusade: Status Passage and the American
           Temperance Movement.* Urbana, IL: The Univ. of Il-
           linois Pr.
   1981   *The Culture of Public Problems: Drinking-Driving and
           the Symbolic Order.* Chicago: Univ. of Chicago Pr.
   1982   "Prevention: Rise, Decline and Renaissance." In *Alco-
           hol, Science and Society Revisited*, edited by E. Gom-
           berg, H. White, and J. Carpenter, 402–25. Ann Ar-
           bor, MI: Univ. of Michigan Pr.

HANFMANN, E.
   1951   "The Life History of an Ex-Alcoholic: With an Evalua-
           tion of Factors Involved in Causation and Rehabilita-
           tion." *Quarterly Journal of Studies on Alcohol* 12:405–
           43.

HARDER, M., J. T. RICHARDSON, AND R. SIMMONDS
   1972   "Jesus People." *Psychology Today* 6:45–50 and 110–13.

HARRISON, M.
   1974   "Preparation for a Life in the Spirit: The Process of Initial
           Commitment to a Religious Life." *Urban Life and
           Culture* 2:387–414.

HEATH, D.
   1962   "Drinking Patterns of the Bolivian Camba." In *Society,
           Culture and Drinking Patterns*, edited by D. J. Pitt-
           man and C. R. Snyder, 22–36. New York: John Wiley
           and Sons.
   1981   "Determining the Sociocultural Context of Alcohol
           Use." *Journal of Studies on Alcohol*, Supplement no.
           9:9–17.

HEATHER, N., AND I. ROBERTSON
   1981   *Controlled Drinking.* London: Methuen.

HEIRICH, M.
   1977   "Change of Heart, a Test of Some Widely Held Theories
           about Religious Conversion." *American Journal of So-
           ciology* 83:653–80.

HILLS, S.
  1977   "Absolutist and Relativist Views of Social Deviance: To-
          ward a Humanistic Perspective." *Human Society*
          1:147–65.

HINE, V.
  1970   "Bridge Burners: Commitment and Participation in a
          Religious Movement." *Sociological Analysis* 31:61–
          66.

HOFF, E. C.
  1968   "The Alcoholisms." Paper presented at the 28th Interna-
          tional Conference on Alcohol and Alcoholism, Wash-
          ington, D.C.

HORTON, D.
  1943   "The Functions of Alcohol in Primitive Societies: A
          Cross-Cultural Study." *Quarterly Journal of Studies on
          Alcohol* 4:199–320.

HURLBURT, G., E. GADE, AND D. FUQUA
  1984   "Personality Differences between Alcoholics Anony-
          mous Members and Nonmembers." *Journal of Studies
          on Alcohol* 45:170–71.

JACKSON, J. K., AND R. CONNER
  1953   "Attitudes of the Parents of Alcoholics, Moderate Drink-
          ers and Nondrinkers toward Drinking." *Quarterly
          Journal of Studies on Alcohol* 14:596–613.

JACOBS, J.
  1967   "A Phenomenological Study of Suicide Notes." *Social
          Problems* 15:60–72.

JELLINEK, E. M.
  1946   "Phases in the Drinking History of Alcoholics; Analysis
          of a Survey Conducted by the Official Organ of Alco-
          holics Anonymous." *Quarterly Journal of Studies on
          Alcohol* 7:1–88.
  1952   "Phases of Alcohol Addiction." *Quarterly Journal of
          Studies on Alcohol* 13:673–84.
  1960   *The Disease Concept of Alcoholism*. New Brunswick, NJ:
          Hillhouse Press.
  1962   "Phases of Alcohol Addiction." In *Society, Culture and
          Drinking Patterns*, edited by D. J. Pittman and C. R.
          Snyder, 356–68. New York: Wiley.

JESSOR, R., T. GRAVES, R. HANSON, AND S. JESSOR
  1968   *Society, Personality, and Deviant Behavior.* New York: Holt, Rinehart, and Winston.

JINDRA, N., AND M. FORSLUND
  1978   "Alcoholics Anonymous in a Western U.S. City." *Journal of Studies on Alcohol* 39:110–19.

JOHNSTON, L. D., J. G. BACHMAN, AND P. M. O'MALLEY
  1981   *Highlights from Student Drug Use In America: 1975–1981.* Washington: U.S. Government Printing Office.

KALB, M., AND M. PROPPER
  1980   "The Future of Alcohology: Craft or Science?" In *Alcoholism: Introduction to Theory and Treatment,* edited by D. Ward, 288–95. Dubuque, IA: Kendall/Hunt.

KANTER, R. M.
  1972   *Commitment and Community: Communes and Utopias in Sociological Perspective.* Cambridge, MA: Harvard Univ. Pr.

KEIL, T., W. USUI, AND J. BUSCH
  1983   "Repeat Admissions for Perceived Problem Drinking: A Social Resources Perspective." *Journal of Studies on Alcohol* 44:95–108.

KELLER, M.
  1972   "The Oddities of Alcoholics." *Quarterly Journal of Studies on Alcohol* 33:1147–48.
  1982   "Alcohol, Science, and Society: Hindsight and Forecast." In *Alcohol, Science, and Society Revisited,* edited by E. Gomberg, H. White, and J. Carpenter, 1–16. Ann Arbor, MI: Univ. of Michigan Pr.

KINSEY, B.
  1966   *The Female Alcoholic.* Springfield, IL: Charles C. Thomas.

KITSUSE, J.
  1962   "Societal Reaction to Deviant Behavior: Problems of Theory and Method." *Social Problems* 9:247–56.

KURTZ, E.
  1979   *Not-God: A History of Alcoholics Anonymous.* Hazelden, MN: Hazelden Educational Services.
  1982   "Why A.A. Works: The Intellectual Significance of Alcoholics Anonymous." *Journal of Studies on Alcohol* 43:38–80.

LAING, R. D.
  1965   *The Divided Self: An Existential Study in Sanity and Madness*. Baltimore: Penguin Books.

LEACH, B.
  1973   "Does Alcoholics Anonymous Really Work?" In *Alcoholism: Progress in Research and Treatment*, edited by P. G. Bourne and R. Fox, 245–84. New York: Academic Press.

LEACH, B., J. L. NORRIS, T. DANCEY, AND L. BISSEL
  1969   "Dimensions of Alcoholics Anonymous. 1935–1965." *International Journal of Addiction* 4:507–41.

LEACH, B., AND J. L. NORRIS
  1977   "Factors in the Development of Alcoholics Anonymous." In *The Biology of Alcoholism, Vol. 5: Treatment and Rehabilitation of the Chronic Alcoholic*, edited by B. Kissin and H. Begleiter, 441–544. New York: Plenum.

LEMERT, E.
  1951   *Social Pathology*. New York: McGraw Hill.
  1954   "Alcohol and the Northwest Coast Indians." *Culture and Society* 2:303–406.
  1958   "The Behavior of the Systematic Check Forger." *Social Problems* 6:141–48.
  1972   *Human Deviance, Social Problems and Social Control*. Englewood Cliffs, NJ: Prentice Hall.
  1981   "Issues in the Study of Deviance." *Sociological Quarterly* 22:285–305.

LENDER, M.
  1979   "Jellinek's Typology of Alcoholism." *Journal of Studies on Alcohol* 40:361–75.

LEVINE, H.
  1978   "The Discovery of Addiction." *Journal of Studies on Alcohol* 39:143–74.

LIFTON, R. J.
  1963   *Thought Reform and the Psychology of Totalism*. New York: Norton.

LINDESMITH, A.
  1947   *Opiate Addiction*. Bloomington, IN: Puncipia Press.

LOFLAND, J.
    1966   *Doomsday Cult.* Englewood Cliffs, NJ: Prentice Hall.
    1969   *Deviance and Identity.* Englewood Cliffs, NJ: Prentice
            Hall.
    1978   "Becoming a World Saver Revisited." In *Conversion Ca-
            reers: In and Out of the New Religions,* edited by J.
            Richardson, 10–23. Beverly Hills, CA: Sage.

LOFLAND, J., AND R. LEJUNE
    1960   "Initial Interaction of Newcomers in Alcoholics Anony-
            mous." *Social Problems* 8:102–11.

LOFLAND, J., AND R. STARK
    1965   "Becoming a World-Saver: A Theory of Conversion to a
            Deviant Perspective." *American Sociological Review*
            30:862–75.

LYMAN, S., AND M. SCOTT
    1970   A *Sociology of the Absurd.* New York: Appleton Century-
            Crofts.

MACANDREW, C., AND R. B. EDGERTON
    1969   *Drunken Comportment: A Social Explanation.* Chicago:
            Aldine Publishing.

MCCAGHY, C.
    1968   "Drinking and Deviance Disavowal: The Case of Child
            Molestors." *Social Problems* 16:43–49.

MCCALL, G.
    1967   "Data Quality Control in Participant Observation." In *Is-
            sues in Participant Observation: A Text and Reader,*
            edited by G. McCall and J. L. Simmons, 128–41.
            Reading, MA: Addison-Wesley Publishing.

MCCARTHY, R.
    1958   "Alcoholism: Attitudes and Attacks, 1775–1925." *Annals*
            315:17.

MCMAHAN, H. G.
    1942   "The Psychotherapeutic Approach to Chronic Alcohol-
            ism in Conjunction with the Alcoholics Anonymous
            Program." *Illinois Psychiatric Journal* 2:15.

MADSEN, W.
    1974   *The American Alcoholic.* Springfield, IL: Charles C.
            Thomas.

MARLATT, G., B. DEMMINGS, AND J. REID
1973   "Loss of Control Drinking in Alcoholics: An Experimental Analogue." *Journal of Abnormal Psychology* 81:233–41.

MARLATT, G., AND D. ROHSENOW.
1981   "The Think-Drink Effect." *Psychology Today* 15, no. 12:60–69, 93.

MARSHALL, M.
1979   *Beliefs, Behaviors, Alcoholic Beverages: A Cross-Cultural Survey.* Ann Arbor, MI: The Univ. of Michigan Pr.

MATZA, D.
1969   *Becoming Deviant.* Englewood Cliffs, NJ: Prentice Hall.

MAXWELL, M. A.
1949   "Social Factors in the Alcoholics Anonymous Program." Ph.D. diss., Univ. of Texas.
1954   "Factors Affecting an Alcoholic's Willingness to Seek Help." *Northwest Science* 28:116–23.
1984   *The Alcoholics Anonymous Experience: A Close-Up View for Professionals.* New York: McGraw-Hill.

MEAD, G. H.
1918   "The Psychology of Punitive Justice." *American Journal of Sociology* 23:577–602.
1934   *Mind, Self, and Society.* Chicago: Univ. of Chicago Pr.

MELLO, N., AND J. MENDELSON
1965   "Operant Analysis of Drinking Habits of Chronic Alcoholics." *Nature* 206:43–46.
1972   "Drinking Patterns during Work Contingent and Non-Contingent Alcohol Acquisition." *Psychosomatic Medicine* 34:139–64.

MENDELSON, J., AND N. MELLO
1966   "Experimental Analysis of Drinking Behavior of Chronic Alcoholics." *Annals of New York Academy of Sciences* 133:828–45.

MEYER, L.
1969   *Off the Sauce.* Garden City, NJ: Doubleday.

MILLER, W.
1981   *Treating the Problem Drinker: Modern Approaches.* Elmsford, NY: Pigamon.
1983   "Controlled Drinking: A History and a Critical Review." *Journal of Studies on Alcohol* 44:68–83.

MILLS, C. W.
   1940   "Situated Actions and Vocabularies of Motive." American Sociological Review 5:904–13.

MINDLIN, D. F.
   1964   "Attitudes toward Alcoholism and toward Self: Differences between Three Alcoholic Groups." Quarterly Journal of Studies on Alcohol 25:136–43.

MIZRUCHI, E. H., AND R. PERRUCCI
   1973   "Norm Qualities and Deviant Behavior." In The Substance of Sociology, edited by E. H. Mizruchi, 304–15. New York: Appleton-Century-Crofts.

MULFORD, H., AND J. FITZGERALD
   1983a "Changes in Alcohol Sales and Drinking Problems in Iowa." Journal of Studies on Alcohol 44:138–61.
   1983b "Changes in the Climate of Authority toward Drinking in Iowa, 1961–1979." Journal of Studies on Alcohol 44:675–87.

MULFORD, H. A., AND D. MILLER
   1959   "Drinking in Iowa: Socio-Cultural Distribution of Drinkers." Quarterly Journal of Studies on Alcohol 20:704–26.
   1960   "Drinking in Iowa IV: Preoccupations with Alcohol and Definitions of Alcohol, Heavy Drinking and Trouble Due to Drinking." Quarterly Journal of Studies on Alcohol 21:279–96.

MYERSON, A.
   1940   "Alcohol: A Study of Social Ambivalence." Quarterly Journal of Studies on Alcohol 1:13–20.

OGBORNE, A., AND A. BORNET
   1982   "Abstinence and Abusive Drinking among Affiliates of Alcoholics Anonymous: Are These the Only Alternatives?" Addictive Behaviors 7:199–202.

PARK, P.
   1973   "Developmental Ordering of Experiences in Alcoholism." Quarterly Journal of Studies on Alcohol 34:473–88.

PARK, P., AND P. WHITEHEAD
   1973   "Developmental Sequence and Dimensions of Alcoholism." Quarterly Journal of Studies on Alcohol 34:473–88.

PARK, R.
  1952   *Human Communities: The City and Human Ecology.*
          Glencoe, IL: The Free Press.

PATRICK, T., AND T. DULACK
  1976   *Let Our Children Go.* New York: Ballantine.

PATTISON, E. M., M. SOBELL, AND L. SOBELL
  1977   *Emerging Concepts of Alcohol Dependence.* New York:
          Springer Publishing.

PENDERY, M., I. MALTZMAN, AND L. WEST
  1982   "Controlled Drinking by Alcoholics? New Findings and
          a Reevaluation of a Major Affirmative Study." *Science*
          217:169–75.

PETRUNIK, M.
  1972   "Seeing the Light: A Study of Conversion to Alcoholics
          Anonymous." *Journal of Voluntary Action Research*
          1:30–38.

PHILLIPSON, M.
  1971   *Understanding Crime and Delinquency.* Chicago: Aldine
          Publishing.

POKORNY, A., AND T. KANAS
  1980   "Stages in the Development of Alcoholism." In *Phenom-
          enology and Treatment of Alcoholism,* edited by W.
          Fann, I. Karacan, A. Pokorny, and R. Williams, 45–
          68. New York: Spectrum Publications.

POLICH, J., D. ARMOR, AND H. BRAIKER
  1980a   *The Course of Alcoholism: Four Years after Treatment.*
          Santa Monica, CA: Rand Corporation.
  1980b   "Patterns of Alcoholism over Four Years." *Journal of
          Studies on Alcohol* 41:397–416.

READ, M.
  1981   "Attitudes of Kentucky Alcohologists: Issues of an Emerg-
          ing Profession." Ph.D. diss., Univ. of Kentucky.

RICHARDSON, J., AND M. STUART
  1978   "Conversion Process Models and the Jesus Movement."
          In *Conversion Careers: In and Out of the New Reli-
          gions,* edited by J. Richardson, 24–42. Beverly Hills,
          CA: Sage.

RICHARDSON, J. T., M. STEWART, AND R. SIMMONDS
  1978   "Conversion to Fundamentalism." *Society* 115:46–52.

RILEY, J. W., C. F. MARDEN, AND M. LIFSHITZ
  1948   "The Motivational Pattern of Drinking." *Quarterly Journal of Studies on Alcohol* 9:353–62.

ROBINSON, D.
  1976   *From Drinking to Alcoholism: A Sociological Commentary.* New York: John Wiley and Sons.
  1979   *Talking out of Alcoholism: The Self-Help Process of Alcoholics Anonymous.* Baltimore: Univ. Park Pr.

ROGERS, J.
  1977   *Why Are You Not a Criminal.* Englewood Cliffs, NJ: Prentice-Hall.

ROHAN, W.
  1978   "Comment on 'The N.C.A. Criteria for the Diagnosis of Alcoholism: An Empirical Evolution Study.'" *Journal of Studies on Alcohol* 39:211–18.

ROIZEN, R.
  1978   "Comments on the Rand Report." In *Alcoholism and Treatment,* edited by D. J. Armor, J. Polich, and H. B. Stambul, 265–75. New York: Wiley.

ROMAN, P. M., AND H. M. TRICE
  1968   "The Sick Role, Labelling Theory, and the Deviant Drinker." *International Journal of Social Psychiatry* 14:245–51.

ROOM, R.
  1970   "Assumptions and Implications of Disease Concepts of Alcoholism." Paper presented at the 29th International Congress on Alcoholism and Drug Dependence, Sydney.
  1976   "Ambivalence as a Sociological Exploration: The Case of Cultural Explanations of Alcohol Problems." *American Sociological Review* 41:1047–65.
  1978   "Governing Images of Alcohol and Drug Problems: The Structure, Sources, and Sequels of Conceptualizations of Intractable Problems." Ph.D. diss., Univ. of California, Berkeley.
  1982   "Alcohol, Science, and Social Control." In *Alcohol, Science and Society Revisited,* edited by G. Gomberg, H. White, and J. Carpenter, 371–84. Ann Arbor, MI: Univ. of Michigan Pr.

ROSE, A.
   1962   *Human Behavior and Social Processes.* Boston: Hough-
            ton Mifflin.
ROTTER, J.
   1954   *Social Learning and Clinical Psychology.* Englewood
            Cliffs, NJ: Prentice Hall.
RUBINGTON, E.
   1973   *Alcohol Problems and Social Control.* Columbus, OH:
            Charles E. Merrill Publishing.
RUBINGTON, E., AND M. WEINBERG
   1973   *Deviance: The Interactionist Perspective.* New York:
            Macmillan.
RUDY, D.
   1977   "Becoming Alcoholic: Accounts of Alcoholics Anony-
            mous Members." Ph.D. diss., Syracuse Univ.
   1980   "Slipping and Sobriety: The Functions of Drinking in
            Alcoholics Anonymous." *Journal of Studies on Alcohol*
            41:727–32.
RUDY, D., AND A. GREIL
   1980   "Taking the Pledge: Mechanisms of Commitment in Al-
            coholics Anonymous." Paper presented at the annual
            meeting of the Society for the Study of Social Prob-
            lems, New York.
SAGARIN, E.
   1969   *Odd Man in: Societies of Deviants in America.* Chicago:
            Quadrangle Books.
SCHATZMAN, L., AND A. STRAUSS
   1973   *Field Research: Strategies for a Natural Sociology.* Engle-
            wood Cliffs, NJ: Prentice Hall.
SCHEFF, T. J.
   1966   *Being Mentally Ill.* Chicago: Aldine Publishing.
   1984
SCHEIN, E.
   1961   *Coercive Persuasion.* New York: Norton.
SCHNEIDER, J.
   1978   "Deviant Drinking as Disease: Alcoholism as a Social
            Accomplishment." *Social Problems* 25:361–72.
SCHUR, E. M.
   1971   *Labeling Deviant Behavior: Its Sociological Conse-
            quences.* New York: Harper and Row.

SCHWARTZ, H., AND J. JACOBS
 1979 *Qualitative Sociology: A Method to the Madness.* New York: Free Press.

SCOTT, M., AND ST. LYMAN
 1968 "Accounts." *American Sociological Review* 33:46–62.

SCOTT, R. A.
 1969 *The Making of Blind Men: A Study of Adult Socialization.* New York: Russell Sage Foundation.

SEIDEN, R. H.
 1960 "The Use of Alcoholics Anonymous Members in Research." *Quarterly Journal of Studies on Alcohol* 21:506–9.

SELTZER, M. L.
 1968 "Michigan Alcoholism Screening Test (MAST), Preliminary Report." *University of Michigan Medical Center Journal* 34:143–45.

SHAFFIR, W., R. STEBBENS, AND A. TAROWITZ
 1980 *Fieldwork: Qualitative Approaches to Social Research.* New York: St. Martins Press.

SHAW, C.
 1966 *The Jack-Roller.* Chicago: Univ. of Chicago Pr.

SHIBUTANI, T.
 1962 "Reference Groups and Social Control." In *Human Behavior and Social Processes,* edited by A. Rose, 128–47. Boston: Houghton Mifflin.

SHUPE, A., R. SPEILMAN, AND S. STIGALL
 1977 "Deprogramming: The New Exorcism." *American Behavioral Scientist* 20:941–56.

SIEGLER, M., AND H. OSMOND
 1968 "Models of Drug Addiction." *International Journal of the Addiction* 3:3–24.

SMITH, P. L.
 1941 "Alcoholics Anonymous." *Psychiatric Quarterly* 15:554–62.

SNYDER, C.
 1958 *Alcohol and the Jews.* Glencoe, IL: Free Press.
 1964 "Inebriety, Alcoholism, and Anomie." In *Anomie and Deviant Behavior,* edited by M. Clinard, 189–212. New York: Free Press.

SOBELL, M.
  1978   "Alternatives to Abstinence: Evidence, Issues and Some
          Proposals." In *Alcoholism: New Directions in Behav-
          ioral Research and Treatment*, edited by P. Nathan, G.
          Marlatt, and T. Loberg, 177–209. New York: Plenum
          Press.

SOBELL, M., AND L. SOBELL
  1978   *Behavioral Treatment of Alcohol Problems*. New York:
          Plenum Press.

SPRADLEY, J.
  1970   *You Owe Yourself a Drunk: An Ethnography of Urban
          Nomads*. Boston: Little, Brown, and Company.

STRAUS, R., AND S. BACON
  1953   *Drinking in College*. New Haven, CT: Yale Univ. Pr.

STRAUSS, R. A.
  1976   "Changing Oneself: Seekers and the Creative Transfor-
          mation of Life Experiences." In *Doing Social Life*, ed-
          ited by J. Lofland, 252–72. New York: Wiley.
  1979   "Religious Conversion as a Personal and Collective Ac-
          complishment." *Sociological Analysis* 40:158–65.

STRYKER, S.
  1964   "The Interactional and Situational Approaches." In
          Handbook of Marriage and the Family, edited by
          H. T. Christensen, 125–70. Chicago: Rand McNally.

SUGARMAN, B.
  1974   *Dayton Village: A Therapeutic Community*. New York:
          Holt, Rinehart, and Winston.

SYKES, G., AND D. MATZA
  1957   "Techniques of Neutralization: A Theory of Delin-
          quency." *American Sociological Review* 22:664–70.

SZASZ, T.
  1966   "Alcoholism: A Socio-Ethical Perspective." *Western
          Medicine Medical Journal* 7:15–21.
  1970   *The Manufacture of Madness*. New York: Harper and
          Row.

TANNENBAUM, F.
  1938   *Crime and the Community*. Boston: Ginn.

REFERENCES 163

TAYLOR, M.
1977   "Alcoholics Anonymous: How It Works. Recovery Pro-
        cesses in a Self-Help Group." Ph.D. diss., Univ. of
        California, San Francisco.

THIO, A.
1978   *Deviant Behavior.* Boston: Houghton Mifflin.

THUNE, C. E.
1977   "Alcoholism and the Archetypal Past." *Journal of Studies
        on Alcohol* 38:75–88.

TIEBOUT, H.
1949   "The Act of Surrender in the Therapeutic Process."
        Quarterly Journal of Studies on Alcohol 10:48–58.
1961   "Alcoholics Anonymous—An Experiment of Nature."
        Quarterly Journal of Studies on Alcohol 22:52–68.

TOCH, HANS
1965   *The Social Psychology of Social Movements.* New York:
        Bobbs-Merrill.

TOURNIER, R.
1979   "Alcoholics Anonymous as Treatment and as Ideology."
        Journal of Studies on Alcohol 40:230–38.

TRAVISANO, R. V.
1970   "Alternation and Conversion as Qualitatively Different
        Transformations." In *Social Psychology through Sym-
        bolic Interaction,* edited by G. Stone and H. Faber-
        man, 549–606. Waltham, MA: Xerox.

TRICE, H. M.
1956   "Alcoholism: Group Factors in Etiology and Therapy."
        Human Organizations 15:33–40.
1957   "A Study of the Process of Affiliation with A.A." *Quar-
        terly Journal of Studies on Alcohol* 18:38–54.
1959   "The Affiliation Motive and Readiness to Join Alcoholics
        Anonymous." *Quarterly Journal of Studies on Alcohol*
        20:313–20.
1966   *Alcoholism in America.* New York: McGraw Hill.
1970   "The 'Outsider's' Role in Field Study." In *Qualitative
        Methodology: Firsthand Involvement with the Social
        World,* edited by W. Filstead, 77–82. Chicago: Rand
        McNally.

TRICE, H. M., AND J. BEYER
1982   "Social Control in Work Settings: Using the Constructive Confrontation Strategy with Problem-Drinking Employees. *Journal of Drug Issues* 12:21–48.

TRICE, H. M., AND P. ROMAN
1970a   "Sociopsychological Predictors of Affiliation with A.A." *Social Psychiatry* 5:51–59.
1970b   "Delabeling, Relabeling, and Alcoholics Anonymous." *Social Problems* 17:538–46.
1972   *Spirits and Demons at Work: Alcohol and Other Drugs on the Job.* Ithaca, NY: Cornell Univ.

TRICE, H. M., AND J. R. WAHL
1958   "A Rank Order Analysis of the Symptoms of Alcoholism." *Quarterly Journal of Studies on Alcohol* 19:636–48.

TROYER, R., B. MARKLE
1983   *Cigarettes: The Battle over Smoking.* New Brunswick, NJ: Rutgers Univ. Pr.

TURNER, R.
1972   "Deviance Avowal as Neutralization of Commitment." *Social Problems* 19:308–21.

ULMAN, A. D.
1953   "The First Drinking Experiences of Addictive and of 'Normal' Drinkers." *Quarterly Journal of Studies on Alcohol* 14:181–91.

VAILLANT, G.
1983   *The Natural History of Alcoholism.* Cambridge, MA: Harvard Univ. Pr.

VIDICH, A.
1955   "Participant Observation and the Collection and Interpretation of Data." *American Journal of Sociology* 60:354–60.

W., BILL.
1967   *As Bill Sees It (The A.A. Way of Life).* New York: Alcoholics Anonymous World Services.

WAGENAAR, A.
1983   *Alcohol, Young Drivers, and Traffic Accidents: Effects of Minimum-Age Laws.* Lexington, MA: D. C. Heath.

WALLGREN, H., AND B. HERBERT
1970   *Actions of Alcohol.* London: Elsevier Publishing.

WASHBURNE, C.
    1956   "Alcohol, Self and the Group." *Quarterly Journal of Studies on Alcohol* 17:108–23.

WHITE, H.
    1982   "Sociological Theories of the Etiology of Alcoholism." In *Alcohol, Science and Society Revisited*, edited by E. Gomberg, H. White, and J. Carpenter, 205–32. Ann Arbor, MI: Univ. of Michigan Pr.

WIENER, C.
    1981   *The Politics of Alcoholism: Building an Arena around a Social Problem*. New Brunswick, NJ: Transaction Books.

WILSON, J.
    1978   *Religion in American Society: The Effective Presence*. Englewood Cliffs, NJ: Prentice Hall.

WISEMAN, J.
    1972   "Sober Time: The Neglected Variable in the Recidivism of Alcoholic Persons." In *Psychological and Social Factors in Drinking and Treatment and Treatment Evaluation*, edited by M. Chafetz, 165–84. Rockville, MD: National Institute on Alcohol Abuse and Alcoholism.

NAME INDEX

SUBJECT INDEX

A.A. *See* Alcoholics Anonymous

Affiliation process with A.A., 18–42; affective bond in the, 39; factors affecting the, 20; interaction in the, 32, 41; quizzes in the, 35; as religious conversion, 32, 34, 42, 135; studies of the, 18–21

Affiliation stages, 21, 42; accepting one's problem, 36–37; first stepping, 26–33, 88, 136; hitting bottom, 22–26; making a commitment, 33–36; telling one's story, 37–40; twelfth step work, 40–42

Alanon, 34, 136

Alcohol: pharmacological effects of, 109, 140; subjective effects of, 120–21, 140

Alcoholic(s): accepting self as, 39, 55, 56; defining self as, 36; hidden, 101–

2; qualifying self as, 23–24, 30, 31. *See also* Qualifying

Alcoholic career(s), 55–69, 108; and contingencies, 60–61; converted, 62–64; convinced, 60–62; pure, 57–60; tangential, 64–66; types of, 66; typology of, 58

Alcoholic characterization(s), 99–106. *See also* Alcoholism

Alcoholic explanation(s), 43–54; as accounts, 47; types of, 44–45; as vocabularies of motive, 44

Alcoholic identity, 64

Alcoholic role(s), 55, 64–66, 103–4; pressure to accept, 103; reasons to accept, 60–61, 101

Alcoholics Anonymous: founding of, 7–8; as a greedy organization, 16–17; historical sketch of, 7–8; ideology of,

David R. Rudy, professor and chair of the Department of Sociology, Social Work and Corrections at Morehead State University, earned his Ph.D. in sociology at Syracuse University. His current research interests include radical identity transformation as well as the social context of drunkenness. Professor Rudy's prior work has appeared in *Qualitative Sociology, Sociological Inquiry, Sociological Focus,* and *The Journal of Studies on Alcohol.*